THE MAGAZINE WRITER'S
HANDBOOK

Millennium Edition

**Other Allison & Busby Writers' Guides
by Gordon Wells**

*The Book Writer's Handbook
The Business of Writing
The Craft of Writing Articles
How to Write Non-Fiction Books
Writers' Questions Answered*

Gordon Wells

The Magazine Writer's Handbook

Millennium Edition (1999/2000)

This seventh edition published in Great Britain in 1999 by
Allison & Busby Ltd
114 New Cavendish Street
London W1M 7FD
http://www.allisonandbusby.ltd.uk

First published by Allison & Busby Ltd 1985
Reprinted 1986
Second edition published 1987
Third edition published 1990
Fourth edition published 1992
Fifth edition published 1994
Sixth edition published 1997

A catalogue record for this title is available from the British Library

ISBN 0 7490 0404 5   332449

Typeset by DAG Publications Ltd, London
Printed and bound in Great Britain by
Biddles Ltd, Guildford and King's Lynn

CONTENTS

Introduction   7
The choice. Payment. Readership. Magazine ranking. The future.
Changes in this seventh edition.

1   The Market Studies   13
An introduction to the layout of the 'report' pages, followed – in
alphabetical order – by market study reports on selected non-
specialist magazines; for each, a full page, reporting on the magazines
content, target readership, best way of approaching the Editor, likely
decision time, likely payment and when to expect it.

2   The 'Best' Markets   87
A subjective assessment, in tabular form, of which magazines are the
best markets for freelance work, based on how many *writer-initiated*
features and short stories they buy per year, and at what price.

3   Who Uses What?   90
The studied magazines listed by types of material used.

4   Literary Magazines   94
Other well-established (paying) markets for short stories and poetry.
How to submit, what they publish, and what they pay.

5   Small Press Magazines   97
A detailed listing – in alphabetical order – of many of the more interesting small-circulation magazines (most produced by so-called
'desk-top publishing' techniques) which publish mainly short stories
and poetry – sometimes for payment. What they publish, the chances
of acceptance and what, if anything, they pay or give contributors.

6   Magazines Excluded – and the Reasons   107
Why some well-known magazines have not been (or are no longer)
included in the Market Studies chapter.

7   Submissions to Editors – The Basic Principles   111
How to submit freelance material to magazine editors, including how
to prepare a query/outline for a feature article and advice on the rights
a writer offers. Three 10-point pre-submission Checklists: Writing
Style; Articles; Short Stories.

8   Writing Picture-Story Scripts   118
The ground rules – for beginners – of an often overlooked writing field.

9   Writing 'Letters to The Editor'   121
How beginners can get into print quickly, and get paid well: the ground rules. The best 'markets' for letters, fillers, tips, etc. – tabulated – with likely payments/prizes.

10   Getting Together   125
Writers' circles. Evening classes. The Writers' Summer School – Swanwick. The Writers' Holiday – Caerleon. Other writers' conferences.

11   Competitions   130
Short story competitions. Poetry competitions.

12   Addresses Useful to the Freelance Writer   133
Remaindered ('bargain') books. Press cuttings. Associations.

13   Updating Market Information   135
Details of three magazine-market information newsletters for writers.

14   The Magazine Writer's Bookshelf   137
Standard reference books. Writing for magazines. Writing style.

15   Word Processing for Writers   139
The equipment. The computer. On the monitor. Storage. Printers. The word processor program.

Index of Magazines   143

Introduction

Successful writing for magazines depends on three things: a good imagination or a knowledge of a particular subject; an ability to put words together; and a knowledge of where to sell one's work – the market. Putting this in another way, success comes from knowing what to write, how to write it, and who to write it for. This handbook is intended to assist writers in selling their work: to help with the essential study of the market, that is, 'who to write it for'.

No handbook can obviate the need for writers to study the market themselves. Any handbook such as this is almost bound to be out of date at least in some details before it can be published. Yet some things about the market change only slowly and this handbook will provide an excellent foundation upon which the writer can build. The wise writer will use it to provide an overall view, a 'first sift', of the market-place – a guide towards the magazines that warrant further, more detailed study.

The choice

There are several hundred magazines and newspapers published regularly in Great Britain and many of these accept material submitted by freelance writers. This handbook considers which, to the freelance, are likely to be the most interesting of these publications. The choice of publications to feature in the main part of this handbook has been based on three considerations, two negative and one positive:

- no need for specialised knowledge;
- no need for localised knowledge;
- payment for publication.

These considerations have led to the exclusion of specialist trade, profession or hobby publications. Who but a pharmacist could write for *The Pharmaceutical Journal* or an aeromodeller for the *Aeromodeller* magazine? And there are many such publications. Of course, this is not to suggest that a freelance writer should not try writing for such publications as *The Pharmaceutical Journal* if he or she is a pharmacist by profession. But a pharmacist will probably know the journal well and will not need the 'first sift' market study that this handbook offers.

Similarly, any freelance writer based in Sussex will – or should – be well aware of the local *Sussex Life* county magazine and be able perhaps to contribute to it. He or she will certainly be less readily able to contribute to *Lancashire Life*. Any freelance who particularly wishes to contribute to a remote county magazine should buy a copy anyway: no handbook will do away with that need.

In further justification of the carefully limited scope of this handbook, the reader is reminded of the wisdom of Samuel Johnson, who pointed out that 'no man but a blockhead' would write without prospect of payment. There is little point in studying a market that does not offer an opportunity to recoup the cost of that study.

The choice of magazine for inclusion in this handbook was based on the considerations listed above. The resultant list can be classified under three headings:

1   **Women's magazines**: overall these are the biggest magazine market, particularly for short stories, but also very much for non-fiction work. (There is a growing tendency though for the women's magazines to prefer commissioning non-fiction themselves – often based on their own, editorial, ideas – rather than choosing from piles of unsolicited submissions. And many magazines now require prior consultation before any submission, even of fiction.)

2   **General interest magazines**: on the whole these tend to be the 'countryside' glossies, or those of that ilk, These are not always the best of payers. Within this category though, there are some of the more widely read women's magazines too, such as *The Lady*.

3   **Leisure interest magazines**: although specialist magazines have largely been excluded, I have assumed that most writers know at least something about doing things in the house and in the garden – and a bit about writing. It is therefore not unreasonable to include a few such magazines. (And, because many non-fiction writers also illustrate their work, the biggest weekly photographic magazine has been included.)

Some of the publications investigated in detail in this handbook accept no fiction; others accept no non-fiction. All of those examined are prepared to consider 'writer-initiated' fiction or non-fiction ideas from freelance writers without editorial 'pull' or the benefit of a famous name – ordinary writers like us. The reports included in the handbook are all based on my own study of the magazines; they are not just editors' blurbs.

For this new edition, the study reports have been thoroughly revised on the basis of fresh sample copies of the magazines; almost all have been completely rewritten. Some of the less relevant magazines have been dropped to make room for new and/or better freelance markets. New magazines are not generally, however, included until they are reasonably established. (A writer cannot extract payment from a magazine that has ceased publication – as I know to my cost.) Each of the reports has been submitted to the appropriate editor and then factually corrected where necessary (but not all editors responded).

Payment

One of the most important things for a freelance to know about a magazine is how much the editor will pay for a writer's work. It is not enough merely to know that the editor *pays*; is the payment *enough*? Does the hire fit the labour? Freelances will wish to decide for themselves whether they are prepared to invest the work needed to research, write, and perhaps also illustrate a feature article for a mere £50, or for a more generous £150, per thousand words. Yet far too many editors still prefer not to disclose this vital and basic information to writers in advance. (Obtaining advance information about payment is one advantage of the preliminary outline approach so often now required.)

However, payments rates are a variable feast: editors will give more for one piece of work than for another; and basic rates tend to increase over the years. Accordingly, all payment rates are quoted in this handbook only by broad groups. Payment rates have been assessed or determined from a number of sources: my own or other writers' experience, published figures, or a general 'feel'. In all cases, editors have been shown the draft reports, including the assessment of payment rates, and have had the opportunity to amend or correct them.

Payment rate groups are listed on page 13.

Readership

In order to sell freelance material to magazines it is important to give the editor what he/she wants. This can only be done with any confidence if the writer has a clear idea of the magazine's readership. If a magazine is directed at teenage girls, it is pointless to try to sell the editor a short story about a grandmother's problems with her two-year-old granddaughter. Even if the story were brilliant, the editor would not be interested because the magazine's readers would not *identify* with the characters.

The easiest way for a freelance to ascertain, with any certainty, the typical reader of any magazine is from the advertisements – and from the readers' letters. Advertising agencies know the media well; they do not advertise their products in a magazine whose readership will not be interested in them.

For that reason, the magazine studies in this handbook include an appraisal of the advertisements as well as of the editorial pages. This appraisal is not in terms of A/B/C1/C2/D type readership – which means much to an advertising man, but little to the average writer – but is in more emotive, meaningful terms. 'Up-market' is not a precise term, nor is 'mail-order shopper', but a readership can readily be pictured from such descriptions. Similarly, the readers' average age is less than precise: advertisers may need this precision, writers do not.

Most of the market-study reports include brief details of a few recent feature articles that the magazine has carried. These are useful in two ways: they indicate the range, or type, of feature that the editor is (or has been) interested in using, and in that sense serve as a model for future submissions; they also provide the freelance writer with ideas for articles on similar subjects that might be offered to other magazines. There need be no worries about plagiarism in 'lifting' such article ideas; the end result will inevitably be very different from the original – and we all borrow ideas.

The market study reports also include details of the regular columns carried by the magazine. These are of importance to the freelance writer for the simple reason that the editor is most unlikely to accept a feature article on a subject usually reserved for the columnist, who is probably paid a regular retainer.

Magazine ranking

As well as the details of the requirements of each magazine, it may also be of interest, and perhaps some use, to the freelance writer to know which magazines – in my very subjective judgement, which is explained later – are 'the best'. A magazine that takes a lot of writer-initiated unsolicited material, even though it may not pay as well as some, is often a very worthwhile market for the 'ordinary' freelance writer to cultivate. In my ranking of the 'best' magazines therefore, I have adopted a system that takes account of the market size as well as the payment rates.

Finally, elsewhere in this handbook there are several short sections on a variety of subjects of interest to the magazine writer. These include an explanation of why some well-known magazines are not featured in the market study reports; advice on how and where to get in touch with fellow writers with similar interests; an extended reminder of how to submit work to editors (which should be common knowledge, but is the sort of thing that editors repeatedly advise writers about); and some elementary advice on writing picture stories. There is also a still further abbreviated chapter on the increasingly commonplace world of word-processing.

The future

Readers – writers and editors alike – are invited to write to the author, c/o Allison & Busby, with any information that will help with future updates of the market study reports (and any other items) in this handbook, in order to make future editions even more helpful. The author would also like to take this opportunity to thank those who commented on earlier editions, or sent information on these and other publications. (If you write to the author, and would like a reply, please enclose a stamped addressed envelope.)

Changes in this seventh edition

The British magazine world is continually changing: new magazines are launched, older ones cease publication. This handbook reflects these changes.

The following magazines, which were included in the 'Market Studies' section of the sixth, 1997/8 edition, have been dropped from this edition.

They have either ceased publication (or been absorbed into other titles), are no longer prepared to consider unsolicited material from freelance writers, or are now, in my view, an insufficient market for 'ordinary' writers.

Freelance Writing and Photography
Just Seventeen
Looks
M & J
New Woman
Parentwise
Quartos (merged with *Acclaim* to become *The New Writer* – see page 54)

The following magazines, either new, newly 'come of age', or newly 'discovered' (or 'rediscovered') by the author, have been added to the 'Market Studies' section of the handbook:

The Big Issue
Brownie
Foreword
Goldlife
Home Run
Kids Alive!
The New Writer
Practical Family History
The Third Alternative

And, of course, all of the magazine 'reports' have been carefully reviewed and updated – entailing considerable re-writing. (They are all based on an assessment of the opportunities for writer-initiated material – i.e., a freelance writer has offered the editor an idea and got a go-ahead, even if only tentative.) Interesting changes in the overall content and style of the magazines reviewed have included, particularly, the continuing shortening of short stories – more and more magazines are going for the 'short-short' – and the enormous increase in the use of readers' 'real-life' stories. (And these personal experiences really are, almost certainly, true stories; several magazines insist on names and addresses and permission to take photographs before accepting any story. This is very different from the 'Confession' stories of some years ago – which were merely 'true-to-life' first person fiction.)

It is also noticeable that still more magazines are specifying 'no unsolicited submissions' in their mastheads – usually in extremely small print. The work of sifting out a few acceptable articles and short stories from much that is unacceptable is becoming uneconomic.

The only way around this state of affairs is to submit advance queries, mentioning or showing copies of your published work, and either follow up with a quick phone call or ... accept that you may not get a reply. Luckily, there are still some publications – often the lower-paying ones – that will consider the work of beginners; and there are always the local, specialist and hobby-based publications for the beginner to sharpen his or her teeth on.

The chapter listing small (or perhaps they should be called 'independent') press magazines has been retained – the format of these magazine entries has been improved in this edition. The list is still far from complete – some editors did not respond to my questionnaire, some because their magazine has ceased publication, and some other magazines have been added – but it is still a useful introduction to a fast-changing population.

Finally, my thanks are due to all the editors of all the magazines who responded so speedily and encouragingly, and who commented so helpfully – and often complimentarily – on my draft market study reports. (Not all editors replied, but most did.) The accuracy of the reports is thanks to the editors; the responsibility for any residual faults rests at my door.

1

The Market Studies

The next seventy-odd pages in this chapter contain the real meat of this handbook: the detailed market study reports of those magazines considered to be the best, most likely outlets for most ordinary, often spare-time free-lance writers – those without any particular area of specialisation. As already explained, the studies do not include specialist trade or hobby magazines, nor county magazines.

The magazine reports are in alphabetical order, the pages set out to a common format. At the top of each page, the magazine's title, beneath it, any message included in their masthead or on the magazine spine. Beneath this, the name of the editor and, where useful/available, the features and fiction editors. The next line gives the group by which the magazine is published, followed by the editorial address and phone and fax numbers. The text of each report also follows a broadly standard sequence of information: target readership, make-up of magazine (editorial and advertising content), regular sections/columns, typical potentially freelance-contributed features and stories, editorial requirements/specifications, and opportunities for fillers, etc.

The 'box' in the top right-hand corner of each sheet gives much information in abbreviated and alphanumeric form. These abbreviations and symbols represent:

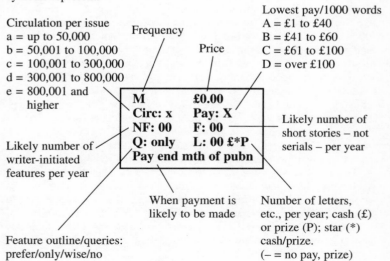

Circulation per issue
a = up to 50,000
b = 50,001 to 100,000
c = 100,001 to 300,000
d = 300,001 to 800,000
e = 800,001 and
    higher

Frequency

Price

Lowest pay/1000 words
A = £1 to £40
B = £41 to £60
C = £61 to £100
D = over £100

M   £0.00
Circ: x   Pay: X
NF: 00   F: 00
Q: only   L: 00 £*P
Pay end mth of pubn

Likely number of
writer-initiated
features per year

Likely number of
short stories – not
serials – per year

When payment is
likely to be made

Number of letters,
etc., per year; cash (£)
or prize (P); star (*)
cash/prize.
(– = no pay, prize)

Feature outline/queries:
prefer/only/wise/no

ACTIVE LIFE
The lively magazine for the years ahead
Editor: Helene Hodge

2M	£2.00§
Circ: c	Pay: C
NF: 70	F: 6
Q: prefer	L: 60 *P
Pay end mth of pubn	

§ on subscription only

Lexi Con *for Post Office Counters Ltd*
1st Floor, 1–5 Clerkenwell Road
London EC1M 5PA

Tel: 0171 253 5775
Fax: 0171 253 5676

Active Life is published by Lexi Con for the Post Office – partly to promote the Post Office's services. As its title suggests, it is a lively publication – its target readership the 'grey panthers', young-in-heart adults of 50+ years, and of both sexes. (The actual core readership is probably nearer their early sixties.) The editor describes the magazine's 'house style' as 'Daily Mail-speak – short and punchy, nothing too long or boring to read.' The over-50s are a prime readership target that everyone wants to reach.

A typical issue of *Active Life* will have 84 colourful saddle-stitched pages of which 40 per cent will be advertisements – the advertisers know how to reach their audience. The adverts are widely varied but with travel opportunities, clothes, pharmaceutical products and ... stair lifts and recliner chairs predominating. There are, of course, several advertisements too for the Post Office's services. As well as the formal advertisements, there are many competitions and reader offers – many free.

On the editorial side much of the magazine is divided up into regular sections or departments: money, law, travel, well-being (health), interests and practical – which includes gardening, cooking and crafts – and people. Within those regular sections there are many actual or potentially freelance-contributed features – about a dozen per issue.

These features range from 250-word 'everyday lives' (one about how an 82-year-old had just 'graduated' from typewriter to word processor) to 500 words on London's Brick Lane Music Hall. (Another short feature dealt with the influx of women MPs – via Emily's List – and, unbelievably, was written by a man.) Apart from the lead story (usually an interview with an appropriately-aged celebrity), which can run to about 1,200 words, most features run out at about 600 words. Most feature articles are illustrated, nearly all in colour, but not necessarily (although it's a 'plus') by the writer; all appropriate feature articles include at least one sidebar (one sidebar per 600 words) – added details, relevant addresses, etc. The editor also particularly asks for a strong 'hook' to start each feature. It's wise to check interest in a feature before submitting it – query first, with a brief outline.

There is a short story in each issue of *Active Life*. This should be around 1,200 words 'on a theme relevant to the readership'. A recent story dealt with inter-family relationships in a residential street: an older lady came to terms with the modern generation. They weren't as bad as she thought.

There is also a lively Letters page in *Active Life* – using about ten longish letters per issue, the best (only) getting an attractive prize and a bouquet.

AMATEUR GARDENING

Acting Editor: Adrian Bishop
Features Editor: Rob Keenan

W	95p
Circ: b	Pay: C
NF: 50	F: NIL
Q: prefer	L: 400 P*P
Pay end mth of pubn	

IPC Magazines Ltd
Westover House, West Quay Road
Poole, Dorset BH15 1JG

Tel: 01202 680586
Fax: 01202 674335

Amateur Gardening is a lively IPC weekly targeted at keen gardeners – most of whom will have ample basic gardening knowledge but are always eager to learn new tricks. The magazine has recently been given a presentational face-lift; it now concentrates on topical gardening articles and expert advice.

A typical issue of *Amateur Gardening* will have just over 50 pages of which maybe a dozen or so will be advertisements – for fertilisers, plants and seeds, for greenhouses, and for various bits of 'essential' garden equipment (no deck-chairs though, for the likes of me). On the editorial side, there are regular (or seasonal) sections dealing with flowers, trees, shrubs and lawns, kitchen gardens, garden birds and equipment tests. There are also regular pages devoted to news, expert advice, what to do next week, and a letters page. There's even a gardeners' crossword puzzle.

The Letters page – address letters to John Negus – uses 8 or 9 non-back-issue-related letters and gardening tips per week, each around 100–150 words: published letters earn a £5 gift token (a £10 token if there's also a photograph used – that is, with about 50 per cent of the letters). The week's best letter and best tip each earn an additional prize – of useful garden equipment. (If you entertain thoughts of contributing features to *Amateur Gardening*, the letters/hints page would be a good place to prove – frequently – that you know your stuff. Get your name known.)

Within the magazine's regular departments/sections there are many freelance contributions – but mostly from a 'stable' of tried and trusted experts (many being well-known 'names' from TV, radio, etc.). There is, though, no reason why an experienced journalist should not contribute successfully: if you have a *relevant* idea, write to the editor with details. Most of the one-off features in *Amateur Gardening* are in the 700-word bracket, packed with facts and often with a sidebar listing contacts, addresses – or step-by-step instruction. One recent feature about daffodils included news of how scientists are improving the strain. And every feature article in the magazine is profusely illustrated – and always in colour.

AMATEUR PHOTOGRAPHER

Views, test and prices every week
Group Editor: Keith Wilson
Deputy and Features Editor: Terry Hope

W	£1.65
Circ: a	Pay: C
NF: 20†	F: NIL
Q: wise	L: 500 *P
Pay end mth of pubn	

† plus many one-off pix

IPC Magazines Ltd
King's Reach Tower, Stamford Street,   Tel: 0171 261 5100
London SE1 9LS   Fax: 0171 261 5404

Amateur Photographer – which was founded in 1884 – is a magazine for ... amateur photographers. (But don't let that word 'amateur' fool you: most readers of *AP* are knowledgeable and up-to-date in their expertise.) Readers of *AP* can be of either sex – with the male of the species undoubtedly in the majority – and their ages probably extend from the late teens to the eighties ... and beyond. Just keen photographers.

A typical issue of *Amateur Photographer* will have about a hundred much-illustrated saddle-stitched pages of which half will be advertisements. There will be a vast number of ads for photographic dealers, all listing cameras, etc., plus several display adverts for new cameras, digital photo scanners (complete with associated computer software), new lenses and the latest colour film. And pages of classifieds offering second-hand cameras, etc.

Editorially, there are many pages of news, views, equipment tests, summarised equipment specifications, and several advice columns. There is a busy Letters page using 10 or more 200-word non-back-issue-related often-illustrated (no pay for these pix) letters each week – with a camera-bag or similar prize only for each week's best.

Inevitably, virtually all of *AP's* regular pages are staff-written. But there are also opportunities for photographers expert in any field to provide one-off features. These are not necessarily illustrated – the magazine holds stocks of readers' photographs – but illustrations are of course welcomed. In one recent issue there was a beautifully illustrated portfolio-with-how-to-advice of flower close-ups. (It's the instructional element that is particularly welcomed – but, of course, you must really know your stuff.) Just about every photograph (other than historic ones) nowadays is in colour.

The editor advises that unillustrated articles should be between 400 and 800 words; illustrated articles can go up to 1,500 words. It would be prudent to check out editorial interest – with a BRIEF outline query – before submitting any feature.

Amateur Photographer also welcome batches of photographs without text – just be sure to include an adequately sized (and stamped) stamped addressed envelope for their return – and don't send more than 20 at a time. You should also confirm in the covering letter that your pix may be held on file for possible future use. They can be transparencies or prints (max size 12 x 16 inches). If you want an acknowledgement of receipt of your pix – send a further sae, and be prepared to wait up to about three weeks. Decisions on acceptability – words and/or pix – can take much longer, so be patient.

BELLA

Editor-in-chief: Jackie Highe
Fiction Editor: Linda O'Byrne

W	60p
Circ: e	Pay: D
NF: NIL§	F: 100
Q: N/A	L: 1000 £*£†
Pay end mth of pubn	

§ many True Life stories
† details below

H. Bauer Publishing
25–27 Camden Road,
London NW1 9LL

Tel: 0171 241 8000
Fax: 0171 485 3774

Launched in 1987 by the German publishers H. Bauer, *Bella* is a bright, breezy, much illustrated and very colourful weekly magazine for women of all ages – but particularly those in their late twenties and early thirties. A typical issue of the magazine will have about 60 saddle-stitched pages of which about a dozen will be advertisements – mainly for food and other household items.

On the editorial side, each issue of *Bella* will have a number of regular sections, covering fashion, beautycare, cookery and home-making – both gardening and interior decorating. There will be pages on legal matters, financial concerns, readers' rights, health ... and news about 'soap' personalities. Inevitably, there are astronomy and 'agony' columns too, as well as a section dealing with bringing up kids. And several Real Life stories.

In common with other similar magazines, the Real Life stories in *Bella* are well paid – £200 a story – and factual. (They really are true stories – offering virtually no opportunity to the 'ordinary' freelance writer.)

However, *Bella* is particularly good for writers of short stories and of letters and tips. There are two short stories in each issue of the magazine. One is a 2,000-word two-pager, often a romance but always told with plenty of warmth, conflict and strong emotional depth – with a 'nice-feeling' ending. The other fiction spot is a one-page short-short story, 1,000–1,200 words long and always with a twist in the final paragraphs. For both fiction spots, detailed study of several sample copies of the magazine is recommended. Address stories to Fiction Editor Linda O'Byrne – and don't expect decisions in less than about six weeks.

For even shorter writers, the magazine welcomes letters, tips, etc., (and ask for a daytime phone number in case they need to get back to you) under:

- 'Precious Moments' – one or two a week, 200 words plus picture, £50.
- 'Snapshot' – anything amusing, just one picture a week, earning £50.
- 'Blush with *Bella*' – embarrassing times, 2 or 3 a week, 100 words, £50.
- 'Tips' – 5 each week, 30–50 words, no pictures, each getting £10. The same payment for the occasional amusing 'Overheard' snippet.
- 'Over to You' – letters, 50–100 words each, 8–10 per issue, £25 for the best, £10 for the rest, no pictures.

best

Editor: Julie Akhurst
Fiction Editor: ???

Circ: d   Pay: C
NF: NIL§ F: 50
Q: N/A   L: 1700£*£†
Pay end mth of pubn

§ many True Life stories
† details below

Gruner + Jahr (UK)
197 Marsh Wall
London E14 9SG

Tel: 0171 519 5500
Fax: 0171 519 5516

A bright and breezy weekly launched in 1987 by one of the leading German publishers, *best* is now well-established on the British scene. A typical issue will have 60 colourful, saddle-stitched pages of which about a dozen are advertisements – for food, pharmaceutical products and special offers, etc. The magazine is intended for women of all ages but its core readership has to be women in their late twenties and early thirties, probably working.

On the editorial side, *best* is, inevitably, in a somewhat similar mould to its competitors – True Life stories and plenty of reader-participation. Regular sections/pages include coverage of fashion, beautycare, health, fitness, and home-making. There are a few pages of recipes, an agony column and, of course, an astrology section. Three or four competitions – crossword variations, with good prizes – are a feature of every issue. Most issues also contain some sort of feature – profile or interview – about a current celebrity and one or two spectacular news stories.

There is virtually no scope for the 'ordinary' freelance non-fiction writer – unless you have (and are willing to reveal) such an 'interesting' life that you can offer several True Life stories. (These stories pay £250 each. Remember though, these really are true stories.)

For short story writers though, *best* is a good market: each issue contains a one-page, 900–1,200-word, short-short story. These don't need to be specifically romances, nor 'twisters' – just good, 'not-instantly-transparent' stories. One I saw was about a girl who conned an 'on-the-make' bloke into acting out her fantasy ... by having him strip naked and going out of her front door, so that she could welcome him arriving in that state. Instead, she left him there.

Letter- and tip-writers too can do well with *best*. Regular slots are:

- 'Letters' – about 15 per issue, up to 100 words each, earning a massive £75 for the best, £25 for the rest.
- '20 New Tips' (address, Tips) – 20 per issue, each 15-30 words long, (photographs not asked for) earning £15 each.

In neither spot are photographs asked for; they do though request a daytime contact phone number.

BEST OF BRITISH
Past and Present
Editor: Peter Kelly

M	£2.40
Circ: a	Pay: A
NF: 200	F: NIL
Q: no†	L: 300 *P
Pay end mth of pubn	

† over 1,000 words – wise

CMS Publishing
Rock House, Scotgate,
Stamford, Lincs. PE9 2YQ

Tel: 01780 763063
Fax: 01780 765788

Best of British was launched by Choice Publications (a joint venture of EMAP and Bayard Presse) in 1994, taken over by an ex-EMAP editor/publisher in 1995, and absorbed into CMS Publishing in 1997. It went from bi-monthly to monthly in 1998. It is – as its title implies – a celebration of all that's best in Britain ... including much nostalgia. Perhaps inevitably, it seems to have a readership of somewhat mature/elderly people – of both sexes.

A typical issue of *Best of British* will have 60 to 70 much-illustrated and colourful, saddle-stitched pages. Of these, almost a quarter will be advertisements – for British memorabilia (plaques, family histories, etc.), holiday opportunities, train models, ornaments and other CMS publications. And several reader offers.

Editorially, there are several regular sections: news of Britain today (what's on, etc.), book reviews, reviews of *old* records and a 'question and answer/contact long-lost-friends' page. As well as those, there are several interesting 'reader-participation' pages: a Letters page using maybe two dozen longish, nostalgic letters a time and giving half-a-dozen (pen) prizes; a 'Poets' Corner' welcoming readers' poems (preferably short, they say, but often running on) but with no mention of payment; and 'Yesterday Remembered'. This latter section invites readers to submit their memories of days gone by: up to 600 words a time, for which they currently pay £20 per item. Typically, 'Yesterday Remembered' items have included school reports, Home Guard cycle patrols, war-time Garrison Theatres, a farmyard childhood, and a business start-up in the late 18th century.

As well as the regular 'Remembered' spot, *Best of British* also features plenty of one-off illustrated articles. The editor writes many of these himself – but there looks to be plenty of freelance opportunity too. Recent feature articles have been about such a range of subjects as the *Eagle* comic, working in a pickle factory, exploring a tiny pub, architectural follies, Meccano models, a reader's collection of book marks, children's annuals, a present-day armour maker and a farewell to the Royal Yacht *Britannia*. All illustrated, mostly in colour – but obviously not when old photographs are essential to the content.

Article lengths are mostly around 1,000 words maximum. Submit the shorter 'Remembered' pieces on spec but it would be wise to get a go-ahead before submitting longer features. Decisions usually within a month.

THE BIG ISSUE
Coming up from the streets
Editor-in-Chief: A. John Bird
Editor: Becky Gardiner
Assistant Editor/Features: Simon Rogers

W	£1.00
Circ: c	Pay: D
NF: 30	F: NIL
Q: wise	L: 250 *P
Pay end mth of pubn	

Fleet House, 57-61 Clerkenwell Road   Tel: 0171 418 0427
London EC1M 5NP

The Big Issue was set up in 1991 to give homeless people the chance to make an income. It is sold on the streets by registered and trained vendors. They do not seek donations, they sell the magazine, which they have themselves bought from the magazine's distribution offices. Its readership is diverse – but it would not be unreasonable to suggest that most purchasers possess a modicum of social conscience. The readership is also particularly interested in what's on in the world of the arts, entertainment, etc.

A typical issue of the magazine will have 48 colour-illustrated-but-not-glossy, 'slightly-better-than-newsprint', saddle-stitched pages of which about 20 will be advertisements. The display adverts are for banks, charities, entertainments, jobs and festivals – and there are half-a-dozen pages (included in the aforementioned 20) of classified ads (for training courses, travel opportunities, jobs ... and telephone chat lines).

Within the editorial pages of *The Big Issue*, there are several regular features: several pages of news, many pages of reviews (clubs, CDs, films, books, etc.), a Letters page (half-a-dozen each week, varying lengths, with a 'Big Issue' courier bag for the weekly best, nothing for the rest), a crossword, and a 'missing persons' page. There are also a number of one-off features each week – often including an interview with a pop-music star or like celebrity. Many of these one-offs are written by *The Big Issue* staff writers, but there are undoubtedly some (well-paying) opportunities for freelance contributions. One potentially freelance contribution recently was a 2,000-word investigation of the stressful life of those engaged in telephone-sales – working in tiny cubicles with their actions continually monitored. There are also opportunities for the homeless themselves to contribute short pieces to the magazine.

It would undoubtedly be prudent to submit a BRIEF outline of any proposed feature article before finalising it. And it is as essential as ever to study the magazine before even putting up an idea.

BROWNIE

Editor: Marion Thompson

M	**£1.20**
Circ: a	**Pay: B**
NF: 48	**F: 12**
Q: no	**L: 80† *P**
Pay end mth of pubn	

† from Brownies only

The Guide Association
17-19 Buckingham Palace Road
London SW1W 0PT

Tel: 0171 834 6242
Fax: 0171 828 8317

BROWNIE is a bright and breezy monthly magazine for Brownie Guides – that is, girls aged 7 to 10. It has been going for more than 37 years and has certainly kept up with the times.

A typical issue of *BROWNIE* will have 32 colourful (there's barely a hint of white page throughout) and saddle-stitched pages. Only one or two pages will be advertisements – for Brownie uniforms and for fun days out.

The magazine is full of colourful double-page spreads. These can be step-by-step words-and-pictures instruction (250 words, in 'steps') on fairly simple things to make with inexpensive materials, short (300-word) factual articles written in illustrated 'info-bite' or 'snippet' form, a short story (500–600 words about a Brownie-related activity), or a picture-story (about Super Brownie – scripted by the Editor). There are pages of picture-puzzles and giveaways, a crowded pen-pal page and a page of readers' letters, poems, drawings or photographs. The best letter, poem, etc., wins a prize.

Editorial guidelines warn against involving Brownies – in stories or how-to articles – in doing anything unsafe or dangerous. They also point out the need for an up-to-date view of family life: today's Brownie could well help dad with the washing up and mum in the garden.

Typical of the craft articles recently has been detailed instruction on making a card, pot-lid and raw carrot Easter 'bonnet', making a lavender sachet shaped like a ... Brown Owl, and how to make a greetings card. Each activity entailed about 6 or 7 steps – each described in about 30 words plus a sketch. If you can't provide an appropriate illustration, a rough sketch will suffice. Recent factual 'articles' – double-page spreads consisting of half-a-dozen 50-word illustrated 'snippets' – have dealt with animal and bird migration, hares and the moon. One recent short story told of the sleepless nights and other problems of a young Brownie – who has a newly arrived baby brother.

The editor of *BROWNIE* particularly welcomes craft articles and sport and hobby information. And a final reminder – not all Brownies are Christians; they can adhere to other religions and faiths.

BUNTY

Editor: J. C. Davie (Mr)

W	65p
Circ: ?	Pay: A
NF: NIL	F: 200 §
Q: yes	L: 400*P†
Pay end mth of pubn	

§ all picture-scripts
† for schoolgirls only

D. C. Thomson & Co Ltd
Albert Square
Dundee DD1 9QJ

Tel: 01382 223131
Fax: 01382 322214

Bunty is one of the several bright and cheerful weekly picture-story comics published by D. C. Thomson: it's been around for over 40 years and having moved with the times is still going strong. It is carefully targeted at school-girls in the 8- to 12-year-old range – top end of primary school, and/or just started at secondary school ... and they grow up fast these days. (Kids like to look ahead – and for this reason, most of the characters in *Bunty* are in their early teens rather than pre-teens.)

A typical issue of *Bunty* will have 32 saddle-stitched pages, three quar-ters in full colour, the rest in black-and-white. There are only a couple of pages of advertisements – for other D. C. Thomson publications. Apart from the stories (see below), there are a number of regular features – an astrology page, 2 pages of puzzles, and a couple of pages of readers' letters. (They use 8 or 9 each week, 50–100 words long and usually illustrated. There's at least one prize for the best letter.) The back cover of each week's issue is usually filled nowadays by a good-looking young male or female celebrity.

There are 7 or 8 picture-stories in each issue of *Bunty*: usually one photo-story and the rest drawn. A couple of the picture-stories will be in black-and-white – the rest, including the photo-story, in colour. There is always a complete (colour, drawn) story about Bunty herself, usually a 9-frame one-pager. (If trying to break into this market, a sample picture-script for the Bunty one-pager seems like a good idea – it might not be accepted, but it would serve to demonstrate your script-writing and story-telling ability.)

In one recent issue, all other picture-stories were within ongoing, often fairly short, serials. At least two stories though – 'The Comp' (Redvale Comprehensive School) and 'The Four Marys' (who attend the surprisingly up-market St. Elmo's boarding school) – are year-after-year favourite regu-lars (although the stories are not that long ongoing). Apart from 'The Comp' which took up four pages in the issue reviewed and 'Bunty', all other pic-stories were three-pagers, varying from 19 (the photo-story) to 23 frames.

If thinking of writing picture-scripts for *Bunty* (and not long ago they were advertising for writers), it is important to remember the constraints. The editor may only want stories about specific characters; virtually all D. C. Thomson characters are the copyright 'property' of the publishers – you can write a story about them for D.C.T. ... but you can't use those charac-ters anywhere else. Study the magazine and check requirements with the editor before offering them material. And remember – you don't have to draw the pictures (see page 118).

BUSINESS OPPORTUNITY WORLD

Editor: John Moulding

M	£2.50
Circ: a	Pay: C
NF: 60	F: NIL
Q: wise	L: NIL
Pay end mth of pubn	

Market Link Publishing plc
The Mill, Bearwalden Business Park,
Wendens Ambo, Saffron Walden,
Essex CB11 4JX

Tel: 01799 544219
Fax: 01799 544205

Business Opportunity World, now published by Market Link Publishing, is aimed at people wishing to start, and successfully run, their own business – and for those who are already making a go of it. It tends to emphasise the franchising and networking aspects of small businesses – without neglecting the possibilities of going it wholly alone.

A typical issue of *Business Opportunity World* will have about 64 glossy, much-illustrated perfect-bound pages – of which half will be advertisements. The advertisements are almost exclusively for franchising and other business opportunities. The editorial pages too have many advertising features – short, fairly interesting articles, often complete with anecdotes, but basically outlining a firm's services.

There are also though, in the editorial pages, plenty of potential freelance opportunities. Many of these, because the magazine is aimed at start-up business people, are how-to guides to business techniques – and not too high-powered. Recent such one-off articles have included a guide to the Internet, advice on selling via the Internet, how to manage your cash flow, what it takes to succeed (by networking), how to avoid paying (any more) late-form penalties to the Inland Revenue, and how, in a one-person business, to delegate! Bearing in mind that every efficient freelance writer is effectively running a small business, articles like these are within the capabilities of many writers (with a relevant specialism). Also within the (non-advertorial) editorial pages, there is occasionally an interview with an interesting business achiever.

Nearly all of the one-off feature articles are about 700 words long with one or two sub-heads; all add a factual sidebar (anything from a bullet-point summary of the article to a list of relevant contacts); nearly all are kept to a well-laid-out single page, most with an artist's illustration, a few, a photograph. One or two features are only half-pagers – about 350 words, unillustrated.

While the editor of *Business Opportunity World* will consider unsolicited articles, it would undoubtedly be wisest to check ideas first, with a BRIEF outline, followed up by a phone call about a week later. And, as always, the magazine needs study before submitting material.

STOP PRESS: Magazine retitled, now PROSPER.

CANDIS
The best magazine for you and your family
Acting Editor: Jenny Campbell
Assistant Editor/Features: David Lloyd

M	£1.80 §
Circ: d	Pay: D
NF: 60	F: 12
Q: prefer	L: 90 P
Pay end mth of pub	

§ subscription £19.50 p.a.

Newhall Publications Ltd
Newhall Lane,
Hoylake, Wirral L47 4BQ

Tel: 0151 632 3232
Fax: 0151 632 5716

Candis is the magazine of the Candis Club and is available on subscription only. The Candis Club has been in existence for more than 35 years; it is dedicated to giving financial support to specific medical charities – they distribute more than £120,000 each month (nearly £40 million has already been given away). The magazine's target readership is Club members – mainly, but not solely, women and generally of a mature age, say, 40-plus.

A typical issue of *Candis* has 120-plus colourful, A5-sized, saddle-stitched pages. Within that there are around 16 pages of adverts – for assorted pharmaceutical products, decorations (plates to figurines) – and a number of special offers. There are also (usually) 9 pages of Candis Club News.

The balance of the *Candis* editorial pages carry several one-off features and a number of regular sections/pages. Regulars include: a celebrity thought for the month, and a couple of opinion columns; sections on antiques, relationships, cooking, gardening, knitting and the environment; and a couple of celebrity interviews – one 'conventional', the other a question and answer feature developed over a lunch-table (titled 'Out to Lunch'). Throughout the magazine there is a slight emphasis on health-related features and sections – understandably so, bearing in mind the Club's charity donations.

There is a regular Letters page, 'Reader to Reader' – mostly back-issue-related letters, 50-100 words a time, each earning a £10 voucher.

Many of the one-off features in each issue are specially commissioned but some could be writer-initiated. It's best to start with a query letter/outline: the editorial staff like to set specific briefs. Obviously, the more important features will be editor-initiated – and use already well-proven writers. Recently-used potentially writer-initiated one-off features have been about the life-styles of three very different 14-year-old girls, a report on a Missing Person Helpline, about life as a football referee today, and a travel article about Normandy. Such features are about 1,000 to 2,000 words long and are illustrated by 4 to 6 colour photographs (usually agency-supplied).

The magazine makes a point of insisting on a high standard of accuracy from its feature-writers. They recommend retaining all research notes, tapes, etc. Most features will be pre-commissioned; if, at the end of the day, through no fault of the writer, the feature is unusable, a 50% kill fee is paid.

There is a 1,000- to 1,500-word short story in each issue of *Candis*. These are often but certainly not always by already published authors, they are often 'nostalgic-romantic' in style, but can be 'straight' or possibly slight 'twisters'.

CAT WORLD
Britain's best-loved cat magazine
Editor: Brigitte Quilter

M	£1.95
Circ: a	Pay: A
NF: 170	F: NIL
Q: phone	L: 40 *P
Pay end mth of pubn	

Ashdown Publishing Ltd
Avalon Court, Star Road,   Tel: 01403 711511
Partridge Green, West Sussex RH13 8RY   Fax: 01403 711521

Cat World changed publishers a year or so ago; it is now an even more attractive glossy magazine packed with super colour photographs of lovely cats – even a centrefold cat pin-up. It is a magazine for all cat lovers with inevitably a slight emphasis on the interests of breeders and 'owners' of 'show cats' rather than ordinary 'moggies'. (Forestalling criticism, the quote marks around 'owners' reflect my awareness that no one 'owns' a cat.)

A typical issue of *Cat World* will have nearly 80 tastefully colourful saddle-stitched high-gloss pages of which almost half will be taken up with advertisements – nearly 20 pages of display ads and around 15 of classifieds. The display advertisements offer everything 'catty' – from cat litter and flea powders to cat insurance, food and charities. The classified ads are mainly taken up with directories of breeders, directories of studs, and a register of cats which have just had kittens (for sale).

Editorially, there are several regular features – a multi-expert problems section, a homeopathic cat-health page, several pages of cat show details and other 'catty' news, and a cat-book review column. There is also a Letters page (inevitably 'Pawpost') using only 3 or 4 long-ish, newsy and illustrated letters per month – the best attracting a small prize.

There are two regular reader-participation spots, 'The cat in my life' and 'Tail end': both one-page, 600-750-word, one or more pix, pet eulogies.

There are also about a dozen other 'non-expert' feature articles in each issue, often particularly-welcomed half-pagers (300–450 words, one photograph) but several stretched to 2 pages by particularly good photographs. (Length of the 2-pagers still didn't exceed about 850 words – just included more good pictures.) Recent subjects for such articles have included the feral cats of Cairo, helping a cat to survive house-moving, the cats of wartime Woolwich arsenal and how to clean out a cat loo. I also saw interesting – particularly so because they could be written by any freelance, not just by a cat-lover – features about cats in cigarette and other trade cards and another on collecting books about cats. *Cat World* welcomes interviews of cat-loving celebrities – or anyone else who's really interesting and out of the ordinary. (They emphasise, they *do not* pay interviewees.)

The editor welcomes really good unsolicited feature articles – but invites prior telephone discussion of the subject. *Cat World* is a popular freelance market – and is therefore often well-stocked. So you might get an acceptance ... and then wait quite a while before publication. No fiction and definitely no poetry.

CHAT

Editor-in-Chief: Iris Burton
Editor: Keith Kendrick
Fiction Editor: Shelley Silas

W	60p	
Circ: d	Pay: B	
NF: NIL§	F: 50	
Q: N/A	L: 3000£*£†	
Pay end mth of pubn		

§ many True Life stories
† details below

IPC Magazines Ltd
King's Reach Tower, Stamford Street
London SE1 9LS

Tel: 0171 261 6565
Fax: 0171 261 6534

A bright and breezy women's magazine from IPC, *Chat* is in direct competition with such German-import magazines as *Take a Break* (page 67) and *that's life!* (page 68). Like them, it is aimed at women of all ages but most particularly at 25- to 45-year-olds – probably working mums with school-age children and limited spare cash.

A typical issue of *Chat* will have 60 colourful saddle-stitched pages full of pictures. About a dozen of the pages will be advertisements – for mail-order catalogues, home ornaments, pharmaceutical products ... and even cigarettes. On the editorial side there are many regular pages/sections covering: fashion, soap gossip, beautycare, fitness, cooking, health, and holidays. There are also the almost obligatory 'agony' and astrology pages. The pages are also full of reader-participation competitions – word squares, crosswords, etc. – with such prizes as 'supermarket dashes', holiday vouchers ... and cash.

Forming a major part of the editorial content of each issue of *Chat* though are the True Life stories. There are usually about half a dozen two-page stories (earning £250 for the person concerned) and a similar number of shorter, under-one-page, stories – which get £100 a time. Be warned though, these really are true stories and feature photographs of the actual people – which means that they offer virtually no scope for the ordinary freelance writer. (Unless your life is truly exciting?)

Chat is though, a good market for short-short stories; they use one in each issue; they are about 950–1,000 words long and are not necessarily romantic or twist-in-the-tail. (One I saw was about a gypsy fortune-teller telling a punter what to bet on to win at the races – and having won, he then lost it all to a pickpocket.) They pay at least £100 a story.

Chat is a particularly good 'market' for the writers of Letters and tips. Opportunities include:

- 'Our tips' – using 24 per issue, about 30 words each, earning £10 plus a fiver for a (relevant) photograph. There's a big prize for the 'Star Tip' too.
- 'Health tips' – half a dozen per issue same length same pay.
- 'Aren't kids cute' – kids' sayings, 10 a week, same length same pay.
- 'Take it away, girls' (Letters) – a dozen a week, most with picture, up to 100 words, £100 for the best, £10 for the rest (plus £5 per piccy).

CHOICE

Britain's magazine for successful retirement

Editor-in-Chief: Sue Dobson
Features Editor: Janet Horwood

M	£2.20
Circ: c	Pay: D
NF: 60	F: NIL
Q: wise	L: 120 P*P
Pay end mth of pubn	

Choice Publications Ltd (EMAP and Bayard Presse)
Apex House, Oundle Road   Tel: 01733 555123
Peterborough, Cambs PE2 9NP   Fax: 01733 898487

Choice is a joint publication from EMAP and Bayard Presse of Paris. It is a lively magazine for lively 55-year-olds (and older), aimed at all those – both men and women – who have not long retired or are about to retire ... and are relatively affluent. (It is a sister magazine to *YOURS* – see page 86. *Choice* readers though are both younger and more affluent than readers of *Yours*.)

A typical issue of *Choice* will have about 120 much-illustrated saddle-stitched pages of which some 35 per cent will be advertisements. The adverts are for such things as recliner chairs and 'mobility scooters', exotic holidays, retirement property and various medications.

Editorially, there are many regular sections and pages in *Choice*. There is always a 12-page centre section on 'Your Rights' – investments, pensions, taxes, etc. Other regulars include sections on health, gardening, cookery, motoring, pets and being a carer. There are a few pages of news and reviews of forthcoming events; there is a reader-service page to help find those with whom readers have lost touch, and a couple of 'problem' pages. There is a lively letters page (write to 'Your Letters') using about ten 100-plus word, some back-issue-related, some not, letters per issue; readers are invited to propound their forthright views or to share their good news. There are prizes for all letters used and a star prize for each month's best.

There are, of course, also a number of one-off feature articles in each issue. A number of these are clearly staff-written or specially commissioned from experts. But there are opportunities for freelance contributions that are relevant to the readership and in the right style.

Typical of such potentially freelance-contributed features have recently included articles about spiritual 'retreats' (holidays for the soul), about the joys of discovering one's roots (family trees) and about getting talking to fellow coach-travellers. There was also a delightful 1,500-word illustrated feature about a river cruise holiday in France; but, like nearly all *Choice*'s travel features, this was staff-written – by the Editor. Most of the other articles mentioned were basically around 700 words long – plus two or three illustrated 'case-studies' averaging around 250 words each. All appropriate features had comprehensive sidebars too – factual information, sources, etc.

Although most articles in the magazine are commissioned, all unsolicited article submissions are carefully read. Much better though: submit an outline first – plus just one or two photocopies of similar published work – and, of course, an s.a.e. Packages of words and (top quality) colour transparencies are particularly welcomed. Decisions normally come quickly.

COUNTRY
*The Magazine of the Country
Gentlemen's Association*
Publisher (=Editor): Tim New

M	£3.50
Circ: a	Pay: C
NF: 40	F: NIL
Q: wise	L: 50 –
Pay end mth of pubn	

The Country Gentlemen's Association
Shuttleworth, Old Warden Park,
Biggleswade, Beds. SG18 9EA

Tel: 01767 626242
Fax: 01767 627158

Country is the magazine of the Country Gentlemen's Association; it is produced in-house, for CGA members. Its readership is obvious – CGA members, i.e., affluent and mature country gentlemen. (It is clearly of interest to their wives too.)

A typical current issue of *Country* will consist of some 56 saddle-stitched pages of which more than half (30-plus) will be advertisements. The adverts reflect the 'country' and the 'affluent gentlemen': they offer country clothing, luxury holidays, garden equipment, stair lifts and retirement homes, and country pictures. The 30-plus advert pages also include ten or a dozen pages of classified adverts – for holiday accommodation, antiques, heraldry, jewellery and the like.

Editorially, there are several regular pages/columns – CGA news and forthcoming social events, advice on travel needs, country books, an occasional Letters page (unpaid, all back-issue-related) and a 'Country Scene' double-page. The 'Country Scene' spread contains five or six filler-like pieces, each about 200 words long usually with a colour illustration. One such recent freelance-contributed filler was about topiary. An ideal 'entry' to the magazine.

In addition to the regular spots there are always several one-off freelance-contributed features in *Country* – often by experts. Recent, more 'ordinary' features have included thoughts on being hard of hearing, an interview with a canal-boat artist, a look at the Queen's pet dogs, an anecdotal report on pig-keeping in Portugal, a plea for more back-garden tennis, and how to ensure care for the elderly. Most such articles are about 700 words long but some stretch to 1,100 words. Nearly all are illustrated with at least one picture, usually in colour.

It would undoubtedly be wise to check feature outlines with the editor/publisher at the CGA before finalising; he responds quickly to BRIEF outlines. Remember the readership and make sure your suggestions are *relevant*. And don't expect a commission, a tentative go-ahead is more than half-way to an acceptance.

COUNTRY LIFE

Editor: Clive Aslet (Ext. 6969)
Features Editor:
Melanie Cable-Alexander (Ext. 6883)

W	£2.25
Circ: b	Pay: D
NF: 20	F: NIL
Q: only	L: 250 –
Pay end mth of pubn	

IPC Magazines Ltd
King's Reach Tower, Stamford Street,
London SE1 9LS

Tel: 0171 261 7058
Fax: 0171 261 5139

Country Life – founded in 1897 – is an up-market weekly magazine with a decidedly affluent readership. The readership is both male and female, probably living in the country, but certainly not strangers to the London scene either. These are mostly stately home or large country estate dwellers, involved in: conservation, the arts, our heritage, country sports, and general good living.

A typical issue of *Country Life* will have about 90 high-gloss perfect-bound pages of which about a half – mostly confined to before and after the editorial material – will be advertisements. About two-thirds of the advertisements are usually for large, expensive country houses and estates; apart from one or two tiny, under-£100,000 cottages, most of the houses are in the £¼m-plus price bracket. Other advertisements are for works of art, antiques, furniture, garden equipment, etc. And there are half-a-dozen pages of classified ads – for property, pets, billiard tables, etc.

Editorially, there are many regular pages/columns – country news, sale-room activities, reviews (books, films, music, exhibitions, etc.), gardening, motoring, fashion, bridge, and sports. There are ongoing series of articles about England's best churches, about 'Country House Treats' (weekend breaks) and a 'Town and Country' collection of 100–200-word country snippets. (They might welcome *relevant* contributions – contact the Page Editor, Camilla Bonn.) There is a non-paying Letters page – write to Correspondence Editor, Rachael Oakden – using four or five mostly back-issue-related, often illustrated letters each week.

There are also usually several one-off articles in each issue of *Country Life*. Many of these are commissioned, a number are by regular contributors or by staff members. But there is some – albeit only little – scope for the experienced freelance with specialist expertise and relevant ideas to contribute. Recent one-off features have included a celebration of the Land Rover's 50th anniversary, an appraisal of South African bulbs and a delight in the non-extinction of the woodlark. Articles vary from about 800 to 1,500 words; illustrations are seldom provided by the writer.

If you have a *relevant* idea for a *Country Life* article, write in, with just a 3- or 4-line synopsis. If they express interest, then follow up with an outline, plus your credentials and photocopies of similar published work. DO NOT phone for a response: they usually respond within a week or so. (They dislike unsolicited phone calls.) But be warned – little unsolicited material makes the grade.

THE COUNTRYMAN
Comes from the country
Editor: Tom Quinn

2M	£2.40
Circ: b	Pay: B
NF: 130	F: NIL
Q: no†	L: 100+ –
Pay end mth of pubn	

† outlines welcomed from repeat
contributors – first-timers send full
manuscript

Sheep Street, Burford   Tel: 01993 822258
Oxon OX18 4LH   Fax: 01993 822703

The Countryman is aimed at the country-lover. The editor will not though, consider any material that sentimentalises about the country, is party-polit-ical, or that unquestioningly promotes field sports. The readership is clearly affluent, middle-aged or older, of both sexes (slightly more male readers than female) and dedicated to enjoying the countryside – although quite possibly living in the town.

A typical issue of *The Countryman* will have 160 much-illustrated perfect-bound A5-sized pages. (There's a picture on almost every page – both colour and black-and-white photographs and the occasional pen-and-ink drawing.) Within the overall 160 pages, 15 to 20 per cent will be adver-tisements – including 8 or 9 pages of classified ads. The adverts – like the contents – reflect the readership: they offer country-wear, accommodation, smokers' necessities, stair-lifts and garden equipment.

Editorially, the magazine carries a number of regular features/columns: country book reviews, gardening advice, readers' collated memories, a country diary and a couple of rather different 'queries answered' spots. There is a page of rural anecdotes ('Tail Corn') and a lively (but unpaid), mostly back-issue-related, Letters page. (The previously often-used multi-page sets of linked photographs are now seldom in evidence.)

But it is for the many one-off feature articles that *The Countryman* is of most interest to the freelance writer. There are 20 or more illustrated articles, of lengths varying from 300 to about 1,500 words, in each issue. Recent subjects have ranged from the history of the ubiquitous 'wellies' to a description of Cornwall's roadside drains (called *leats*); from a look at some of the famous 'named' oak trees in Sherwood Forest to the wife sellers of old Charlbury and the long-vanished cattlemen of Wales. If it's about the country – and well written – your article could interest the editor.

The editor welcomes article outlines/queries from previous (successful) contributors but prefers finished manuscripts from first-time article-writers. Illustrations are always welcome, with the articles. Be warned though – there is much competition for publication in *The Countryman* – the editor only takes the best. Decisions on outlines and completed submissions usually come within a month.

COUNTRY QUEST
Your magazine for Wales and the Borders
Editor: Beverley Davies

M	£1.80
Circ: a	Pay: A
NF: 180	F: NIL
Q: no	L: 80 –
Pay end mth of pubn	

Cambrian News (Aberystwyth) Ltd
7 Aberystwyth Science Park
Aberystwyth, Ceredigion SY23 3AH

Tel: 01970 611611
Fax: 01790 612505

Country Quest is much like a big English county magazine but is aimed at readers throughout the whole of Wales and the Border counties. (It is this broad regional interest which justifies its inclusion in the *Handbook*. Ordinary county magazines are outside my self-imposed terms of reference – see Introduction, page 7.) The magazine's readership is clear – people of all ages (but predominantly those of mature years) of both sexes, living in, or having a particular personal association with, the area.

A typical issue of *Country Quest* will currently have 64 saddle-stitched pages, mainly black-and-white illustrated, of which about a third will be advertisements. The adverts are for a wide variety of products – reflecting the diverse nature of firms operating within the readership area – including a few tourist-oriented products (e.g., Welsh love-spoons) and reader offers. Editorially, there are one-off articles and regular columns. Regulars include local-interest book reviews, an antiques section, a feature on 'interesting' cars and a Letters page. (Half-a-dozen or so longish letters per month, mostly back-issue-related – no pay.) There is also a poetry page – about three a month, 'traditional/conventional' in style – titled 'Poetry Corner'.

But it is for its one-off features that *Country Quest* is of most interest to the freelance writer. There are always a lot of such one-offs – as many as 15 or so per issue – and almost certainly all initially unsolicited. Inevitably, these are about people, places, customs, traditions and events associated with the readership area – Wales and the Borders.

Recent such articles have included a history of a small, family-owned North Wales bus company, a review of the history and traditions of St. David's Day, the legend of a South Wales gnome (*Pwka'r Trwyn*), the background story of a well-known painting (of Salem Chapel), and a description of typical Welsh peasant cottages. Most articles are 2-pagers and about 80 per cent are illustrated (mostly in black-and-white).

The Editor advises that one-page feature articles should be around 700 words, two-pagers, 1,400. Original illustrations are welcomed: if provided, deduct 200 from the preferred wordages. (*Country Quest* will accept black-and-white prints, or colour prints, transparencies or negatives.)

Country Quest uses no fiction. Decisions come fairly quickly. Deliver/submit date-related material at least two months before issue date.

DOGS MONTHLY

Editor: Ruth Chapman

M	£2.35
Circ: a	Pay: A
NF: 30	F: 10
Q: no	L: 140 –
Pay end mth of pubn	

R.T.C. Associates
Ascot House, High Street
Ascot, Berks. SL5 7JG

Tel: 01344 891797
Fax: 01344 622771

Dogs Monthly is a magazine about dogs, for dog-owners: predominantly, but not exclusively, for specialist breeders or 'show-ers'; it is also for those with ordinary family pets. The common factor is that the readers are all dog-enthusiasts, dog-lovers. The magazine has been established now for about fifteen years.

A typical issue of *Dogs Monthly* will have 70 to 80 pages, of which just under a third are advertisements – for dog clubs, dog foods, dog insurance policies, dog training ... anything 'doggy'. It also contains, within the advertisements, much information on dog-breeders – a Breeders Directory.

On the editorial side – always well-illustrated – there are usually several pages of news – new products, dog club activities, competitions – several of specialist dog-care advice and a few of 'doggy' book reviews. There is a regular Letters page – but no pay or prize.

But in each issue there are also one-off feature articles which dog-owning freelance writers might aspire to contribute. But you really need to know your subject. Typical of such one-offs might be advice on caring for older dogs, advice on insuring your dog, or general information about the life of a police dog.

There is also an occasional opportunity for an 800-word short-short (non-shaggy) dog story 'of real quality'.

The Editor is willing to discuss article ideas or to see unsolicited articles in their finished form. Decisions come within a month.

ESSENTIALS

Editor-in-chief: Sue James
Editor: Karen Livermore
Features Editor: Debbie Attewell (Ext. 7697)

M	£1.80
Circ: d	Pay: D
NF: 30	F: NIL
Q: only	L: 60 £*P
Pay end mth of pubn	

IPC Magazines Ltd
King's Reach Tower, Stamford Street,
London SE1 9LS

Tel: 0171 261 6970
Fax: 0171 261 5262

Essentials is a glossy magazine filled with practical advice on a wide range of topics. It is aimed at women in their mid-30s and over, almost certainly in some form of stable relationship, probably with primary-school-age children – and a keen family/home-maker. The typical reader may well juggle job (maybe part-time) and family – and while enthusiastic about making things herself she doesn't always have much time.

A typical issue of *Essentials* will have about 160 saddle-stitched pages (plus a bound-in paper pattern for a dress or whatever). About a third of the pages will be filled with advertisements – for beauty products, for pharmaceutical products, for foodstuffs and for a variety of other goods, from washing up liquid to fancy telephones. There are also (included in the advertisement pages) several pages of classified ads offering a range of services from cosmetic surgery via maternity clothes to telephone chatlines.

On the editorial side, there are a number of regular sections – a dozen or so pages on fashion, health and beauty, parenting, home-making (from DIY to re-furnishing), travel and cooking (I noticed, 'The World's Shortest Recipes'). Each month, about a dozen centre pages are designed to tear out and save – they're hole-punched already, for filing. There is an astrology column and a couple of 'agony' columns. And a Letters page using half-a-dozen or so, 150–200-word, mostly back-issue-related (and/or 'look at what I made from your pattern'), letters per month. Everything published gets £20 and the best gets a £100 box of cosmetics.

There are not a vast number of opportunities for the 'ordinary' freelance to contribute one-off features to *Essentials* – they have staff feature writers – but there are some. There is a regular 'Boys at the Back' spot of about 700 words – a recent one dealt with the traumas of first-fatherhood (from first announcement to delivery). And there are two or three other potentially freelance-contributed features in a recent issue – a 400-word, 9-bullet-point advice on coping with income tax and another, 200 words on something to give the kids to do in the holidays.

If you have a really *relevant* idea for an *Essentials* article, send the editor a BRIEF outline and keep your fingers crossed. You could try phoning the Features Ed after about a week.

FAMILY CIRCLE

Editor: Sue James

M	£1.30
Circ: d	Pay: D
NF: 25	F: NIL
Q: only	L: 100 P*P
Pay end mth of pubn	

IPC Magazines Ltd
King's Reach Tower, Stamford Street,   Tel: 0171 261 6195
London SE1 9LS   Fax: 0171 261 5929

Family Circle is a bright, cheerful monthly magazine from IPC. At one time, it was sold almost exclusively in supermarkets – but not (any more than dozens of other magazines) nowadays. As its title implies, it is aimed at family-based women – aged, say, 28 to 45 – sometimes with a part-time job, often with children at secondary school.

A typical issue of *Family Circle* will have about 140 colourful, saddle-stitched pages of which a quarter will be advertisements – many for food-stuffs and pharmaceutical products, but also for cosmetics, household equipment, etc. There will also be a number of special reader offers – short holidays, household equipment, etc.

Editorially there are several regular sections: home-making and personal life-style, family life, health, beauty, fashion and cookery. There may be a dozen or so pages of *relevant* fashion; there will almost always be about 20 pages of mouth-watering (and quick-to-prepare) recipes – plus several more pages on supermarket best food buys. There is a crossword, a 'Stars' page, a travel section, and a small Letters (and hints) page. The Letters page uses 8 or 9 letters (100 words, most not back-issue-related, pix welcomed) and tips each month, giving a £10 M&S voucher for each and a bouquet too, for the best. (Write to 'Get in touch', *Family Circle*.)

The magazine is not at all enthusiastic about unsolicited articles. (Currently they use fiction only occasionally – but 'this may become more regular'.) In the masthead they say:

> 'We are rarely able to use unsolicited manuscripts and readers should keep their own copies. ... we do our best to return [manuscripts] if stamps are enclosed but cannot guarantee this.'

Nevertheless, some of their features could, potentially, have been produced by experienced freelance writers. Typical of possible *potential* freelance material were a short 6-point article about getting a job at 40+, a consideration (with anecdotal quotes) of how some topics are still taboo in front of Mum (of any age), and a travel piece about a less-well-known aspect of Florida. (The travel page is always *assembled* in-house.)

If you think you have an idea for a *relevant* feature for *Family Circle*, submit a BRIEF outline (plus just one or two photocopies of similar published work if possible) and await editorial interest.

THE FIELD

Editor: Jonathan Young

M	£2.80
Circ: a	Pay: D
NF: 40	F: NIL
Q: only	L: –
Pay end mth of pubn	

IPC Magazines Ltd
King's Reach Tower, Stamford Street,
London SE1 9LS

Tel: 0171 261 5198
Fax: 0171 261 5358

The Field is a glossy, well-illustrated monthly magazine from IPC. Founded in 1853 as a weekly paper for gentlemen, it has changed its frequency but not its target readership. This is largely, but not exclusively, male – and undoubtedly affluent. It caters for the real country-person rather than those with a sentimental fondness for the *idea* of the country. Field sports have always been central to its interests – and most other 'gentlemen's activities' are also covered.

A typical issue of *The Field* will have 100-plus much-illustrated pages of which about a third are advertisements – for country properties, guns and gun accessories, outdoor clothes, country-house furniture, jewellery and antiques. On the editorial side there are many regular sections/pages – covering property, gardening, cookery, motoring, country events, the theatre, bridge and chess.

There are plenty of one-off features too – and the editor welcomes the opportunity to consider really *Field-relevant* feature ideas. Something out of the ordinary, yet within the areas of interest, would be the best bet. But submit only BRIEF, written, article outlines – and only if you have the appropriate expertise. Illustrations are usually commissioned – but those who can offer complete 'packages' of (expert) words and (really good quality) pictures are always welcomed. You might try phoning (be brief and business-like) after about ten days to enquire about interest in the outline.

One-off features (anything from 800 to 2,000 words long) in *The Field* have included illustrated articles about greyhound racing, Romanies, the Somerset eels, cemeteries across Europe, bell-ringing and the Norfolk terrier. A broad 'field' of interests.

There is also a regular section in *The Field* called 'Out in the Field' that previews forthcoming country events, exhibitions, etc., and includes date-relevant snippets (200–300 words) – in February, for example, a 250-word history of pancakes. Such snippets are often freelance-contributed. A good opening if you can produce what they want.

FOREWORD
The Writers' Club Magazine
Editor: Paul Diner
Address all correspondence,
submissions, etc. to:
The Secretary (Susan Green) at ...

2M	£2.50 §
Circ: a	Pay: B
NF: 45	F: NIL†
Q: prefer	L: 50
Pay: mth after pubn	

§ notional price – subscription only,
£36 pa: – incl monthly newsletter
† but comp. in each issue

Foreword Magazines
Park Terrace East
Horsham, West Sussex RH13 5DJ

Park Terrace Courtyard,
Tel: 01403 210074
Fax: 01403 249948

Launched in late 1996, *Foreword* offers subscribers a range of facilities, including advice, manuscript appraisal, discounts on seminars, writers' services and relevant books – and two very different magazines. *Foreword* is one – an illustrated, high-gloss, art-paper bi-monthly magazine. The other is a monthly newsletter, *Market News for Writers* – for more on which, see page 135. All the services, facilities, magazines, etc. are covered by the one subscription of £36.

A typical issue of *Foreword* will contain 24 saddle-stitched pages (including the cover) – none of which are advertisements. The regular features are steadily being built up; at the time of writing there is a page for poets, a two-page 'Masterclass' (on techniques), a page about writing courses, a Letters page ('Members Forum' – no payments, no prizes) and a tail-end chat column ('And another thing ...'). Each issue of *Foreword* also includes a prizewinning short story (plus the judges' report on the best few entries) – and details of the next competition.

Significantly, each issue of *Foreword* has a particular theme. Recent issues have dealt, in depth, with Poetry, Romance Writing, Publishers, Writing for Children, and Article-writing. Themed issues include one-off articles by acknowledged experts in their fields. These expert one-off articles are often well-illustrated too – one on writing comic script included reproductions of the sketchy initial 'storyboard', the submitted script ... and the published picture-story. Other one-offs have included a two-pager on the US Romance market, a look at the history of words, a two-page review of the small presses, and a look at income tax as it applies to writers.

Articles are best queried before submitting – but you will only get a tentative go-ahead until the finished work is submitted; preferred lengths are: one page, 900–1,100 words; two pages, 1,600–1,800 words – anything longer should be pre-agreed. To get an acceptance, you must really know what you're writing about. Once a written acceptance of the article is received, *Foreword* requires an invoice for the agreed fee – currently £50 per page. Payment is about one month after publication. No invoice, no payment. Decisions on queries and finished work come quickly – but some accepted articles are then held over for an appropriately themed issue.

GEOGRAPHICAL

The Royal Geographical Society Magazine
Editor-in-Chief: Fiona McWilliam
Features Editor: Claire Hutchings

M	£2.75
Circ: a	Pay: D
NF: 25	F: NIL
Q: only	L: 80†
Pay end mth of pubn	

† geographical Q+As P*P

Campion Interactive Publishing Ltd – for RGS
47c Kensington Court   Tel: 0171 938 4011
London W8 5DA   Fax: 0171 938 4022

Geographical is the magazine of the Royal Geographical Society; it was founded in 1935. It is mainly targeted at members (Fellows) of the Society but is clearly of interest to many other 'lay' readers and is readily available from larger newsagents. It is edited and produced, on behalf of the Royal Geographical Society, by Campion Interactive Publishing Ltd.

A typical issue of *Geographical* will consist of 100 colourful glossy perfect-bound pages of which about 30 per cent will be advertisements. The adverts reflect the readership – offering outdoor clothing, cameras, watches and other essential items of travellers' equipment, books about travel ... and destinations.

On the editorial side there are a number of regular sections/features: geographical news and views from around the world, reviews of relevant new products ('gadgets and goodies'), a look ahead at what's (going to be) on, a detailed geographical guide to a specific area of Britain, and even a crossword. There is a non-paying, mostly back-issue-related, Letters page (write to 'Points of View') using four or five longish letters per issue and a 'Questions and Answers' page offering prizes for all interesting questions and readers' answers – using half-a-dozen or so per issue.

Each issue of *Geographical* also has maybe 7 or 8 one-off feature articles. Most of these are contributed by well-known explorers or academics in the geographical field, or are written in-house, but two or three features in each issue are usually by experienced freelance writers. Typical of such one-offs have been features on London – 'hooked' to the introduction of a new-style mayor – and on the poverty and politics of Nicaragua. Both these articles were about 1,800 words long, lavishly colour-illustrated (one writer-illustrated, one not).

If you have detailed geographical knowledge or recent experience of a specific area – and can formulate this as a *relevant* feature idea – it would be worth submitting a detailed outline to the editor. Don't waste time with ideas for travel articles without geographical content though. Be warned – it's got to be really good to get a go-ahead.

GOLDLIFE

The magazine for 50-Forward members

Editor: Nimita Parmar

2M	£2.50
Circ: a?	Pay: D
NF: 45	F: NIL
Q: only	L: 25 *£
Pay end mth of pubn	

Affinity Publishing Ltd
2nd Floor, 1-5 Clerkenwell Road
London EC1M 5PA

Tel: 0171 251 5489
Fax: 0171 251 5490

First published in 1989, *Goldlife* – the magazine for 50-Forward members – is available by membership subscription only. It is another bright, breezy, magazine, accurately targeting the attractive over-50s age-group – of both sexes.

A typical issue of *Goldlife* will have about 70 colourful saddle-stitched pages of which around 20 will be display advertisements; the adverts offer attractive holidays, healthcare goods, insurance policies, gardening aids, etc. (And the almost inevitable stairlift.) All, reflecting the interests and needs of the over-50 readership.

Editorially, *Goldlife* has a number of sections within which both regular features and one-off contributions are accommodated. There are sections covering health, travel, finance, 'interests' and gardening. Within the sections are regular features including various news pages – over-50 interests, travel, health, finance, shopping, etc. – a couple of regular opinion columns, a cookery section, reviews of books and videos and a double spread of crosswords and other puzzles. There is usually an interview feature – of an over-50 celebrity. There is a Letters page using four or five 100-word letters per issue – from subscribers only, of course – the best winning £25. *Goldlife* does not use fiction.

It is, though, for its one-off feature articles that *Goldlife* is of most interest to the freelance writer. A few of these are staff-written but most are freelance-supplied. All fit within the magazine's standard 'sections' (above). They are also interested in the occasional 'nostalgic' article – disappearing occupations, how life has changed, etc.

A recent issue had illustrated articles about a day out at a wildfowl park in Sussex, exploring an artists' village in France, and the delights of fly fishing. There was advice on using a variety of unusual pots in the garden, how to make up and display hanging baskets, enjoying an off-the-beaten-track holiday in Spain and a report on coping with mastectomy – and several more. Most of the features are two-pagers (1,000 words max), all are colour-illustrated (not all by the writer, although words-and-pix packages are much appreciated), and almost all include factual sidebars (sources, etc.). One-page features too are usually illustrated and can be up to 800 words long.

Clear article ideas with the editor before proceeding; when submitting, they require a disk as well as the usual double-spaced typescript.

GOOD HOUSEKEEPING
The best of everything
Editor-in-Chief: Pat Roberts Cairns
Features Editor: Marilyn Warnick

M	£2.20
Circ: d	Pay: D
NF: 50	F: 0/12†
Q: only	L: 70 P*P
Pay on acceptance	

† from comp. winners or
commissioned 'names'

National Magazine Company Ltd
National Magazine House,
72 Broadwick Street, London W1V 2BP

Tel: 0171 439 5000
Fax: 0171 439 5591

Good Housekeeping has been around for 75 years – and is still in the fore-front of quality magazines for women. It is well-aimed at the relatively affluent woman in her early forties; her interests are closely aligned to home and family life although, nowadays, many will also have careers.

A typical issue of *Good Housekeeping* will have 250-plus glossy, perfect-bound pages of which about a half will usually be advertisements. The display adverts are for clothes, cosmetics, furnishings, kitchen equip-ment, food, etc. There are usually about a dozen pages of classified ads too – for everything from cooking courses and cosmetic surgery to holiday accommodation and water softeners. And, within the editorial pages, there are always many reader offers.

Editorially, *Good Housekeeping* has a number of regular multi-page sections or departments: homes and gardens, health, fashion and beauty, travel and a couple of comment columns (one by Maureen Lipman) – plus the predictable astrology, reviews and a Letters page. (Write to 'You Write to Us' – there are about half-a-dozen, approximately 100-word, letters a month, almost all back-issue-related, each getting a phone-card and the best (currently) attracting a super BT pager.) And of course, in each issue there are the 'Good Housekeeping Institute' pages – two dozen or more pages of succulent Institute-tested recipes and 8 or 9 pages of consumer reviews.

There is a 'straight' (non-genre) short story – of about 2,500 words in each issue of *Good Housekeeping* – three prize-winners from their annual competition, the rest commissioned from well-known authors.

There are also half-a-dozen or so one-off feature articles in each issue, clearly written by freelance writers, some with well-known names. Recently, the potentially *ordinary*-freelance-written articles have included a review of the life of a full-time mum (with four kids), a commentary on women's predilection for long, chatty phone-calls, a piece about the decline of the dinner party and a explanation of why some men prefer older, more mature, women. Each of these articles was between 1,200 and 1,600 words long; each of them included several relevant quotes – from 'ordinary' people; and none was writer-illustrated.

If you have an idea for a suitable – human interest, health, personal growth/improvement – feature for *Good Housekeeping*, send in a BRIEF well-thought-through outline/query. And await the response – within 2 to 3 weeks. You could get a (possibly non-committal) go-ahead.

HERITAGE
A Celebration of Britain
Editor: Siân Ellis
Art Editor: Paul C. Tutill

2M	£2.95
Circ: b	Pay: C
NF: 20	F: NIL
Q: always	L: 40 –
Pay end 2nd pubn mth	

Bulldog Magazines Ltd
4 The Courtyard, Denmark Street
Wokingham, Berks. RG40 2AZ

Tel: 01189 771677
Fax: 01189 772903

Heritage is an up-market glossy magazine, beautifully illustrated on virtually every page, portraying all that is best and most colourful in British life, history and the countryside. Its target readership is of both sexes, well educated, undoubtedly affluent and largely middle-aged. There are many North American readers too: in the USA and Canada it is published as *Realm*.

A typical current issue of *Heritage* will have 80-plus perfect-bound pages of which about two dozen will be advertisements – including half-a-dozen pages of classified ads. Most of the advertisements are for places to visit in Britain – days out or longer holidays – and where to stay, but there is also a sprinkling of adverts for clothing, jewellery, and ... ancestor research/tracing. Editorially, there are a number of regular sections/pages: news and comments on what's on, a series of profiles of Great Britons, an opinion spot and a travel guide; even a quiz. And a Letters page – using half-a-dozen per issue, up to 150 words each – but with no payment.

Of more importance to the freelance writer, there are also several one-off features – 6 or 7 – in every issue. Most of the features are about 1,200 words each – but the many illustrations mean that they often spread over several pages. A feature on the delights of central England had 20 colour photographs and filled 7 pages. Other recent features have included a review of the 'Century of Change' (7 pages, 21 pictures – nostalgia and ephemera); and a magnificently illustrated 6-page feature about Liverpool – with 11 superb photographs, one or two filling near double-page spreads. Somewhat more down-to-earth, there was a shorter, 2-page feature on ships' figure-heads – with 10 photographs, most reproduced at near thumbnail size.

Don't submit anything on spec to *Heritage* – apart from anything else, a worthwhile feature may entail considerable research. But the editor is always happy to consider *relevant* outlines/ideas. Submit queries by post, then try to catch the sometimes elusive editor by phone a week or so later: once 'caught', decisions come quickly. (The Editor's secretary, Andrea Stone, will always take messages.)

Having raved about the illustrations in *Heritage*, don't be put off by your possible inability to produce quality photographs (colour transparencies, at least $2\frac{1}{4}$ inches square – no black-and-white at all, except historical). Most features are illustrated by other than the writer – by agency or 'on-call' photographers. If you can though, produce high quality photographs you'll give yourself an edge. Complete words-and-pix packages are always preferred. If you can't provide photographs, picture *ideas* are also helpful.

HOME & COUNTRY
Journal of the National Federation of Women's Institutes
Editor: Amber Tokeley
Features Editor: Julia Davis

M	£1.45
Circ: b	Pay: C
NF: 100	F: NIL
Q: prefer†	L: 100 *P
Pay end mth of pubn	

† not for Almanack items

NFWI
104 New King's Road
London SW6 4LY

Tel: 0171 731 5777
Fax: 0171 736 4061

The official journal of the National Federation of Women's Institutes, *Home & Country* is mainly available on subscription through local WI branches but can also be ordered through newsagents. Inevitably, contributions from WI members will have an edge over those from non-members – but outside contributions (including *relevant* material from men) are welcomed. The readership of the magazine is obvious: WI members – relatively affluent, largely middle-aged women with broadly country/rural lives and/or interests.

A typical issue of *Home & Country* will have about 70 colourful (but not brash) saddle-stitched pages of which roughly one third will be advertisements – half and half, display and classifieds. The display adverts offer pharmaceutical products, country-ish clothes and day-out suggestions; the classifieds are mainly for B&B accommodation – from Land's End to ...

Editorially, the magazine of course includes about a dozen pages of WI news, features and 'business'. There are regular sections dealing with food and cooking, gardening, health, book reviews and travel; there are usually a few pages of craft instruction. (One such feature was on how to make yourself a stationery folder. If you have ideas for this spot, contact the Craft Editor, Clare Royals.) There is a lively Letters page using about 10 often back-issue-related letters, 1-200 words each, with a prize for the best.

As well as the regular features, there are a good number of one-off articles, some – but by no means all – from WI members. Subjects range from rural and environmental issues to travel, pets and hobbies. Recent freelance contributions have included a series on a Land Rover trek to Tibet and back, a look at present-day customer service, and a day out at a stately home. There was also an interesting feature about houses and places associated with favourite writers – from Hardy's Wessex to Shakespeare's Globe and the Dylan Thomas Centre in Swansea. Articles should not exceed 1,000 words and where appropriate there is always a fact-packed sidebar. Illustrations will always be welcome but clearly some are agency-provided. It's best to query feature ideas before submitting – to confirm interest.

One other regular feature of the magazine is the 'Country Almanack' section edited by Sue Scott. Short (300–400-word, too short to pre-query), ideally colour-illustrated, *on spec* contributions on 'News, thoughts and lore on our environment and rural life' are particularly welcomed. Recent items have included the use of leeches as weather forecasters, the decline in Britain's bat population, the beauty of the giant hogweed and 'How to photograph garden birds' – with evidence of the contributor's success.

HOME RUN
For all who want to work effectively
Alone or from a small office
Editor: Sophie Chalmers

10 p.a.	£7.20 §
Circ: a	Pay: C
NF: 60	F: NIL
Q: only	L: –
Pay end mth of pubn	

§ subscription only: £72 pa

Active Information
Cribau Mill, The Cwm, Llanvair Discoed,   Tel: 01291 641222
Chepstow, Gwent NP6 6RD   Fax: 01291 641777

Home Run is a magazine 'specially written for people who want to make money while enjoying the freedom of working for themselves from home or in a small business.' It is only available by subscription – expensive but worth it. The magazine is recognised by the media – press, radio and TV – as an authority on micro businesses.

A typical issue of *Home Run* will consist of 24 fact-packed pages with virtually no illustrations (other than thumbnail pix of some contributors) and little more than one page of advertisements – for home business services, etc. The outside cover pages are taken up with news and information on matters relating to professional home-workers and small businesses – new equipment/programs/services. In each issue there are usually articles – not necessarily regular columns – dealing with marketing, personal development, tax and employment issues, plus columns on legal and technology matters.

The bulk of the magazine is full of knowledgeable, eminently practical and down-to-earth one-off articles about how readers can do better at, or start up, their home business. The back issue index includes articles on business 'angels', self-publishing, body language, tax self-assessment, telephone selling, and the true cost of a letter. A vast diversity of linked interests.

Typical recent articles have included 700 words on how to design an effective brochure, about 2,000 words on where to look for good but cheaper-than-expected professional help – graphic artists, photographers, etc., and 1,200 words on how to succeed as an inventor (this was effectively a case study of a patent application). The editor likes case studies – readers learn from others' hindsight.

Despite the 2,000-word article mentioned above, the editor prefers articles to be within the range: 500 to 1,500 words. All articles have many subheadings (about every 100–200 words) and inevitably a fact-filled sidebar. Many of the articles in the magazine favour the easily-assimilated '7-steps' or '5 sins' format.

In all, about half a dozen articles per issue look to be freelance-contributed. BUT – initially the editor wants only ideas, in writing. She responds quickly to every letter and – perhaps after discussing interesting-looking ideas – will commission suitable articles. Articles (and preliminary ideas) are best when tightly focused – with detailed advice – rather than general surveys with little insight.

And don't forget – freelance writing is a one-person home business: *Home Run* is directed at people just like us.

HOMES & GARDENS

Editor: Matthew Line

Features Editor (Acting): Caroline Suter
(Ext. 6181)
IPC Magazines Ltd
King's Reach Tower, Stamford Street,
London SE1 9LS

M	£2.40
Circ: c	Pay: D
NF: 35	F: NIL
Q: only	L: –
Pay end mth of pubn	

Tel: 0171 261 5678
Fax: 0171 261 6247

Homes & Gardens is stylish, and dedicated to ... homes and gardens. It is targeted mainly – but not solely – at women: artistically house-and-garden-proud, sophisticated and affluent, probably in the 35- to 55-year age bracket.

A typical issue of *Homes & Gardens* will have 180-plus glossy perfect-bound pages – plus (in the London editions only) a bound-in 24-page (three-quarters advertisements) supplement detailing what's available in the capital's shops. Of the magazine *proper*, about forty per cent of the pages will be advertisements – for furniture, carpets and curtains, household equipment and fittings, and garden furniture ... and some food items. There are also occasional additional bound-in advertising sections – carpets, etc.

Editorially, the pages are lavishly illustrated. There are regular sections/departments dealing with houses, gardens, decorating and cooking. There is an advice page: you pay to ask a question. There are always several pages of news of current exhibitions too.

Undoubtedly, most of the one-off articles in each issue of *Homes & Gardens* are staff-led commissioned features: for most of those about house interiors the photographs are 'styled' as well as photographed. But there are usually potential opportunities for freelance writer-initiated features too. There are occasional travel articles – usually about 500–600 words long with both words and pix often by the writer – recently, one on walking in Spain. I noticed too, a 6-page feature about a 'natural' garden – 800 words and 8 superb photographs, some full-page: if you know of an interesting garden, you could get an editorial go-ahead. (Interestingly, they commission the words *after* they commission the pix.) Another potentially freelance-initiated feature was about a young couple who, moving into a larger home, furnished it entirely by mail order. (About 600 words – pix not by the writer.)

If you have a really *relevant* feature idea, suitable for *Homes & Gardens* – submit a BRIEF written outline. You could get a go-ahead. But no unsolicited finished manuscripts. Try a quick phone call about a week or ten days after sending in an outline, to check its fate.

IDEAL HOME

Editor-in-Chief: Isobel McKenzie-Price

M	£1.80
Circ: c	Pay: D
NF: 15	F: NIL
Q: wise	L: 70 P*P
Pay end mth of pubn	

IPC Magazines Ltd
King's Reach Tower, Stamford Street,
London SE1 9LS

Tel: 0171 261 6474
Fax: 0171 261 6697

Nearing 80 years old, *Ideal Home* is still going strong and thriving; it is another of IPC's 'quality' magazines. Despite the increased competition in 'home' magazines, it remains one of Britain's leading home-interest publications. Its readership is undoubtedly affluent, fashionably house-proud and often slightly 'way-out' trendy; predominantly female, it is broadly in the 25–45 age group; and probably loyal.

A typical issue of *Ideal Home* will be thick, chunky and perfect bound; the pages are much illustrated and always colourful, but 'brash' it's not. The many advertisements will cover a wide range of home equipment: bedding, kitchens, bathrooms, and lots of furniture – both trendy and traditional.

The editorial pages are full of lavishly illustrated features about lovely homes and gardens and about furnishing them; there are pictures of flowers, and of gardens and their 'fixtures and fittings'; there are advice articles on home maintenance and on cooking; and there are 'reader offers'. There is a Letters page – write to 'Letters to the Editor' – using around half-a-dozen mainly back-issue-related longish contributions each month; published letters earn a prize with a star prize for the best. There is little scope for the non-specialist feature offering; most main features are staff-written or specially commissioned.

Most issues of *Ideal Home* do, however, also contain one or two short articles that *could* be provided by a competent freelance. Such articles though, must of course be accurately targeted at the up-market readership. The Editor is willing to consider full manuscripts on spec – but you'd be much wiser to write in first with a query/outline. No fiction, of course.

Not a big market, but 'a good one to be seen in'.

THE ILLUSTRATED LONDON NEWS

Editor-in-Chief: Alison Booth

2-3 pa	£2.50
Circ: b	Pay: D
NF: 10	F: NIL
Q: only	L: –
Pay end mth of pubn	

20 Upper Ground
London SE1 9PF

Tel: 0171 805 5555
Fax: 0171 805 5911

The Illustrated London News has been published since 1842, bringing readers the news in pictures since long before the days of *Picture Post, Life* or *Paris Match*. Today though, its news content is limited to just a few pages within the magazine. It is a very glossy, very up-market publication, now only appearing two or three times per year, with many illustrations to support its general-interest feature articles. The readership of *The Illustrated London News* is (or dreams of being) in the Rolls Royce/Savoy Hotel bracket.

A typical issue of *The Illustrated London News* will have about 100 glossy, perfect-bound pages of which about a quarter will be advertisements – for top-quality wines, the 'better' spirits, up-market cars, jewellery ... and exclusive hotels. On the editorial side, a typical issue will carry perhaps six or seven multi-page, much-illustrated feature articles. These have included such one-off features as an interview with Shirley Temple Black, profiles of some of Britain's young music makers, an article on the Heritage of London Trust, another on the Hubble Space Telescope, and one on Britain's young chess prodigies. There is also often an up-market travel feature.

Apart from the one-off features, *The Illustrated London News* has a staff-written few-months-ahead look at what's to come in the world of entertainment.

Overall, it's not a good market for the 'ordinary' freelance. There are few opportunities for wholly unsolicited feature articles, but if you have a *relevant* idea and know how it should be worked up to fit their needs/style, the Editor will be happy to consider it – and decide quickly. If you do get a tentative go-ahead or a commission (and someone has to), great. But don't hold your breath. It's a prestigious, and well-paying, place in which to be published.

INTERZONE
Science Fiction and Fantasy
Editor: David Pringle

M	£3.00
Circ: a	Pay: A
NF: 5	F: 70
Q: no	L: 20 –
Pay end mth of pubn	

217 Preston Drove   Tel: 01273 504710
Brighton, East Sussex BN1 6FL

Possibly the last monthly fiction magazine – in any genre – still being
published in Britain, *Interzone* has survived and flourished for more than
130 issues – since 1982. It is a well-produced, well-illustrated, professional
yet totally independent publication: it receives just a small Arts Council
grant. In the world of SF, it is internationally renowned; it is the only British
magazine to have won the prestigious Hugo award.

Interzone's readers are science fiction/fantasy fans. It is a specialist-
interest fiction/fiction-related magazine at 'the cutting edge'. It's not a
magazine to offer 'any old weirdo story' to; its requirements are specific
and its style needs to be studied. (It's way past Robert Heinlein and Anne
McCaffrey yet not into the stranger realms of some SF 'fanzines'.) It's
essential to read several issues before submitting anything – or you'll be
wasting everyone's time.

A typical issue of *Interzone* will have about 70 pages of which only
about 4 will be advertisements – mainly for publishers' new SF/fantasy
books. Editorially, there are several regular columns/sections: film and TV
reviews, several pages of book reviews, an author interview and an SF-
world gossip column (incomprehensible to outsiders). The editor – who has
an encyclopaedic knowledge of SF – occasionally allows himself to offer
his views in a lengthy editorial: alternatively the space is given over to
readers' letters. And then there is the fiction. There are five or six SF or
fantasy stories in most issues; many are by big names (recently Tanith Lee
and Sarah Ash) but the editor is always on the look-out for new talent.

In his guidelines, the editor says, 'We are looking for innovative, entertaining, well-written and up-to-date science fiction and fantasy. We are
unlikely to accept hackneyed space opera, sword-and-sorcery tales, or
traditional ghost stories.'

Stories should be within the range 2,000 to 6,000 words (mark the
wordage on the cover sheet) – no short-shorts, no novellas; send only one
story at a time; get the layout right – paras indented, no line-space between
paras, good wide margins and no 'dotty' typescript. Don't staple the pages,
use a paperclip; don't use padded bags, cardboard folders or anything that
hinders postal delivery and increases postal costs. As well as the essential
MS-sized s.a.e., send a stamped addressed postcard if you want acknowledgement of receipt. *Interzone* buys First English-Language Rights
(i.e., including American); decisions take *at least* two months.

KIDS ALIVE!

Editor: Captain Ken Nesbitt

W	20p
Circ: a	Pay: A
NF: 50†	F: 50†
Q: wise	· L: NIL
Pay on acceptance §	

† mostly picture-stories
§ send invoice

The Salvation Army
101 Queen Victoria Street
London EC4P 4EP

Tel: 0171 332 0022
Fax: 0171 236 3491

Previously known as *The Young Soldier*, the Salvation Army's children's newspaper has now become *Kids Alive!* (It is the UK's only weekly children's Christian newspaper and – under both names – has been going since 1881.) Its target readership is obvious – all children, aged about 7 to 12. It is, of course, Christian based and often educational – but the content is not all religious and is never heavy-handed. (It's rather like a cheerful Sunday school in print.)

A typical issue of *Kids Alive!* will have 12 colourful outside-advert-free A4 pages. The first two pages are usually newsy – the second page being activity news from young readers and a star-prize letter (leave this to the kids). Thereafter, there are usually several whole-page (8- to 10-frame) picture-stories: one, always a Bible story and another, a straightforward comic story. Sometimes there are also picture-story serial stories – one suggested, in a story, how to deal with bullies at school – and sometimes one-off picture-script articles (about interesting people, for example). Most of the picture-stories are freelance supplied – writers provide a script only (see advice on page 118), the magazine arranges the artistry.

There is always a double-page centre-spread of puzzles, word searches, jokes, etc., interspersed with a couple of regular 'conventional' three-frame comic strips and a regular Bible-text-related cartoon. There is often a cartoon-illustrated science or other experiment for readers to do for themselves; or something to make. There is often a thought-provoking competition – for interesting prizes. And there is always a 'Postal Sunday School Weekly' page carrying a 300- to 350-word moral-pointing story. If you can tell a typical Sunday school story, you could try writing one of these.

The editor of *Kids Alive!* welcomes small puzzles for the centre pages, and prior suggestions for fiction and non-fiction pic-scripts. It is, though, even more essential than usual to study the magazine before submitting – it's *different*. Ask for free back issues and contributors guidelines. It's a small and busy editorial office but decisions usually come fairly quickly. Nice people.

THE LADY

The very special weekly magazine
Editor: Arline Usden
Assistant Editor (for Features):
Lindsay Fulcher
Fiction Editor: Beverly Davies

W	70p
Circ: b	Pay: C
NF: 270	F: 50
Q: not needed†	L:NIL
Pay end mth of pubn	

† but check 'anniversaries'

39-40 Bedford Street
London WC2E 9ER

Tel: 0171 379 4717
Fax: 0171 836 4620

The Lady was founded in 1885 – and is still going strong. Over the years, its content has changed somewhat – but slowly. Its readership, though, has not changed much – they are readily identifiable as gentle, affluent and 40-plus.

A typical issue of *The Lady* will have about 90 saddle-stitched pages, some black-and-white illustrated, some colour. Of the 90 pages, nearly two-thirds will be filled with advertisements: about 20 of these are display ads for such things as holiday houses and hotels, nursing homes, charities, clothes, flowers ... and stairlifts. The rest of the advert pages will be *The Lady*'s renowned classified ads – for holiday houses and hotels (in the UK and abroad) for domestic staff ... and it is THE place for nannies.

Within the editorial pages there will be a number of regular features each week: news of current concerts, exhibitions, etc., advice on gardening and shopping, a couple of pages each of recipes and fashion, a 'readers' queries answered' page and part-pages on bridge, crosswords and the 'Ladygram'. Celebrity interviews and a back-page 'Favourite Things' feature are also regulars. There will also be several one-off feature articles and a short story.

More of the articles are staff-written now than in the past but there are still 5 or 6 weekly opportunities for freelance contributions. There is a useful opinion spot, 'Viewpoint' – reader-contributed, possibly controversial (but religion and politics are barred) and up to about 500 words long. (I saw one recently on the pros and cons of bypasses.) 'Viewpoint' apart, *The Lady* welcomes one- or two-page articles (900- and 1,200-word respectively, and ideally with 2 to 3 black-and-white print or colour transparency photographs per page) and uses 4 or 5 per issue. One recent issue had 2-page interview-based articles about a well-known children's author and a British composer, details of a famous 'stately home' and a review of the delights on show at a current art exhibition. Advance query/outlines are welcomed, but are not necessary – except for potential anniversary-based articles, in case someone else has got in first.

The weekly short story is a *Lady* innovation. Some come from their annual £1,000 competition but you can also submit on spec at any time. Competition details and the essential entry form are (usually – you'll have to watch out for it) in the first issue of *The Lady* in October and entries have to be in by mid-November. It would be a good idea to study some *Lady*-published stories in advance, to get your ideas sorted out.

Decisions on articles and article-ideas can take several weeks – and then there's often a delay before publication. But they're pleasant to work with.

MIZZ
Life, lads and laughs!
Editor: Lucie Tobin
Features Editor: Julie Burniston

2W	£1.25
Circ: c	Pay: C
NF: 40	F: NIL
Q: only	L: 400P*£†
Pay end mth of pubn	

† leave to teenage readers

IPC Magazines Ltd
King's Reach Tower, Stamford Street,
London SE1 9LS

Tel: 0171 261 6319
Fax: 0171 261 6032

Mizz is a bright and resolutely cheerful fortnightly magazine for young teenaged girls, predominantly in the 12 to 15 age group. The readers are interested in, and get lots about, just what the 'shout line' suggests – '*Life, lads and laughs!*' They get loads of poster-pictures of boys – 'tottie' – too.

A typical issue of *Mizz* will have about 90 colourful, saddle-stitched pages of which only 8 or 10 will be advertisements – for cosmetic and hygiene products (and chocolates). The pages are all more picture than text. The text is often no more than lengthy, supposedly hand-written captions and speech-balloons to the cartoon characters or photographs. Where a feature *is* text-based, the words are all in a number of useful-but-brief (150-200 words each) 'info-bite' boxes. (Like sidebars but without the 'main' text.)

Editorially, each issue of *Mizz* will have regular beauty-care and teenaged fashion sections, plus lots of pages of show-biz news and gossip. And the aforementioned half-dozen 'cool' poster-pictures of 'gorge' blokes. There are astrology and puzzle pages and a sympathetic problems page complete with a problem – and answer – converted (by the agony aunt) into a photo-story. There is much reader-participation: a lively Letters and tips page (all short, all reader-only, paying up to £20) and a 'Cringe' page (embarrassing moments – e.g., accidentally displaying one's pink knickers [*Advice: 'Here's £1.50; go and buy some white Granny-knickers.'*] – again, earning up to £20). No scope here for the letter-writing freelance – leave it to the kids.

Most one-off features in *Mizz* are produced in-house or by a regular 'stable' of proven freelances. But there is some scope for the newcomer: *Mizz* uses several real-life stories (particularly child heroes) in each issue. These are interview-based stories about 400–500 words each. If you spot an interesting-looking report in your local newspaper – and you've done similar work before – it would be worth asking the editor if you could interview the (young, boy or girl) teenager and write up their story.

Other one-off features in *Mizz* include such things as quizzes ('How stoopid are you?') and 'special reports'. One freelance-contributed double-page spread looked at the less-than-marvellous lives of some circus animals. If you have an idea for a feature that will really interest and concern young teenagers, send the editor a BRIEF outline – by post – with just one or two samples of your previously published work, and keep your fingers crossed. You might then try phoning after about ten days, to check reaction.

More!
Smart girls get ... more!
Editor: Marina Gask
Fiction Editor: Nigel May

2W	£1.25
Circ: d	Pay: D
NF: NIL	F: 25
Q: N/A	L: 100 *P
Pay end mth of pubn	

EMAP Elan Ltd
Endeavour House, 189 Shaftesbury Avenue,   Tel: 0171 437 9011
London WC2H 8JG

Aimed at girls in their late teens to early twenties, *more!* is bright and cheerful, much illustrated and packed with all the things that interest girls in that age bracket. As well as articles about hunky men, sex and relationships, topics such as travel, emotional issues and careers are also covered.

A typical issue of *more!* will have about 100 pages of which about 30 will be advertisements – for cosmetics and similar products, for clothes, and other things of interest to young women. There are also about 20 pages of fashion and cosmetic advertorial – teenage models displaying various outfits with details of where they are available and the cost.

On the conventional editorial side, the magazine has a number of (staff-written) real-life stories, photo-sessions-cum-interviews with pop groups and hunky stars, and a number of colourful staff-or-commissioned features about men's 'pulling' abilities and the like. Much of the magazine is written in a light, jokey, sometimes sexually suggestive, style.

There is an astrology column, a couple of 'agony' pages (one by an 'agony uncle', one by an 'aunt'), and a Letters page (half-a-dozen letters per issue with a £20 voucher for the best, nothing for the rest). There is also a multi-page 'Excess' section dealing fairly explicitly with sexual matters – and including a well-illustrated, rather uncomfortable-looking 'Position of the Fortnight' complete with 'Difficulty rating'. (It was though, said to be worth the effort.)

Nowadays, there is not a lot for the 'ordinary' freelance writer in *more!* About 40 per cent of the features are commissioned – from a group of well-proven freelances – but they are always willing to consider *relevant* ideas on spec. And there is a regular short story, billed as *erotic*. By today's standards – Black Lace, etc. – I would class it as relatively mild eroticism. Preferred length is about 800 words – a real short-short.

MOTHER & BABY
UK's best-selling baby mag
Editor: Melanie Deeprose

M	£1.70
Circ: b	Pay: D
NF: 10	F: NIL
Q: only	L: 70 £*P
Pay end mth of pubn	

EMAP Élan Ltd
Endeavour House, 189 Shaftesbury Avenue,   Tel: 0171 437 9011
London WC2H 8JG   Fax: 0171 208 3584

Mother & Baby magazine has been around for more than 40 years (it was founded in 1956) and all the while has kept itself well and truly up-to-date. It is all about ... motherhood and babies – and toddlers up to about three years old. Its target readership is obviously young mums and mums-to-be: it offers reassurance, advice and information.

A typical issue of *Mother & Baby* will have 148 breezy, colourful, saddle-stitched pages of which more than 60 will be advertisements. The ads are for child-care pharmaceuticals, baby and toddler food – and clothes for both mother and baby – and many *sensible* toys (for toddlers and dads).

Editorially, the magazine has a number of core sections – dealing with pregnancy and birth, bringing up babies and toddlers, development, health and consumer testing. Within those departments there are many one-off features, often by specialist experts but with the possibility of some being by experienced freelance writers. (I noticed the name of one 'case study' mother also getting a byline for an article on how to cope with twins.).

There are regular 'My Story' features, written in the first person, about a mother's experience of a difficult health problem – either related to herself, or her baby/toddler. Articles are usually around 1,200 to 1,800 words but can go to over 2,000; all have factual sidebars and sources of further advice/information. Illustrations are not by writers.

If you have what you think is a relevant idea for a feature in *Mother & Baby*, send the features editor a BRIEF outline and some evidence of your parental and writing credentials. If you get a go-ahead, the features editor will specify the style and angle the feature should take in order to fit in with future editorial requirements.

Mother & Baby also has a lively Letters page: up to half-a-dozen letters about previous features, mums' views and funny anecdotes, up to 150 words plus a (non-returnable) baby-pic – they pay £10 each with a prize for the month's best. They also welcome 'cringe-worthy' experiences – and 'anything to make us laugh' – for the end-of-mag 'Back-chat' page (address to 'The Last Word') and offer various prizes (cosmetics, films, etc., worth about a tenner) for each item used. The magazine also invites readers to share their birth stories – and pays £15 a time.

Overall, if you're a young mum or mum-to-be, and a writer, then *Mother & Baby* is worth a look – but there's not a lot of scope for grandads like me.

MY WEEKLY
The magazine for women everywhere
Editor: Harrison Watson
Fiction Editor: Ian Somerville
Features Editor: Sally Hampton

W	50p
Circ: d	Pay: B
NF: 100	F: 100
Q: prefer	L: 600 £*P
Pay on acceptance	

D. C. Thomson & Co Ltd
80 Kingsway East
Dundee DD4 8SL

Tel: 01382 223131
Fax: 01382 452491

My Weekly has been around since 1910 – and is still going strong. Its readership is, as its sub-title says, 'women everywhere'. The target reader age is probably women in their mid- to late-forties but it is undoubtedly read by women from their mid-twenties to their sixties and beyond.

A typical issue of *My Weekly* will consist of about 55 to 60 saddle-stitched ages of which as many as 20 will sometimes be advertisements. The adverts reflect the readership – stair-lifts, recliner chairs, mail-order clothes, plates and the like, to hang on the wall and plants and equipment for the garden. House-proud but careful with their money.

The magazine has a number of regular features or columns, including: health, cooking, knitting or other patterns and fashion. There is the inevitable astrology column and an agony column; there is a crossword and gossip about the 'soaps'. Like many other magazines today, *My Weekly* also has a reader-participation True Life story spot: 'Your Own Page', which offers £50 for a story about 'a special time you'd like to share' – about 800–900 words long. Not of much interest for the freelance writer though.

Most issues carry one or two interview-based features though – in one issue there was a two-page feature about the *Peak Practice* characters and another (about 1,600 words long) on the hectic life of the boss of the Filey lifeboat. These look like freelance-written – but query first.

There is a lively Letters page (including some tips) too. Write to 'Your Letters, *My Weekly*, 185 Fleet Street, London EC4 2HS – and they ask you, when writing, to tell them your 3 favourite items in the magazine (which makes it difficult for non-readers). They use about a dozen letters of up to 150 words each and pay £3 for each one used – with a good extra prize for the best of the week.

But it is for its fiction that *My Weekly* is best known. In one recent issue the lead serial was by Catherine Cookson – some competition! But serials apart, the Fiction Editor is in the market for short-short stories (1,000–1,500 possibly off-beat, occasionally twist-in-the-tail, words) and for longer stories up to 4,000 words (with 2,500 words being ideal). Story characters can be any age as long as they're *real* and the stories entertaining. (One story I saw was about a couple about to celebrate their silver wedding anniversary: both planned a surprise holiday – but each different. The news of a forthcoming grandchild solved the dilemma – they abandoned all holiday ideas.)

Decisions on article queries and short stories come within 6 to 8 weeks. If you're 'nearly there' the people at DCT are well-known for being helpful.

NEW CHRISTIAN HERALD
Your bold new voice
Editor: Russ Bravo
Features Editor: Jackie Stead
News Editor: Karen Carter

W	55p
Circ: a	Pay: B
NF: 300	F: NIL
Q: wise	L: 400 – †
Pay end mth of pubn	

† – see below, no payment

Christian Media
96 Dominion Road
Worthing, West Sussex BN14 8JP

Tel: 01903 821082
Fax: 01903 821081

A tabloid-sized weekly newspaper, *New Christian Herald* is aimed at evangelical Christians, both sexes, all ages – but perhaps concentrating its attention most on 25- to 45-year-olds. Throughout, it is written in a lively, bright and contemporary style – committed, but with a sense of humour. It says its design style is 'Daily Mail meets Daily Mirror'.

A typical issue of *New Christian Herald* will consist of 20 newsprint pages of which the first half-dozen are filled with news about church and evangelical matters. Within the paper there are no more than about 3 pages of advertisements, 70 per cent classified, the rest display: it's particularly good for church-related job ads, for holiday accommodation ads and there are always display ads for charities, etc.

After the news pages come plenty of pages of features – some staff- or regular-contributor-written, and often news-related. Particularly suitable for, and open to, the religious freelance are interviews with Christian celebrities and other believers working in the religious and entertainment field – one issue contained an interview with a committed children's author and another with a religious broadcaster. Preferred length for features is 650 to 800 words; they also use some half-page features of up to 400 words.

There are also short reviews – of books relevant to readers' faith, of books suitable for children, and of CDs (everything from Gregorian chants to pop groups and gospel singers). These reviews are usually about 200 words each; in a recent issue there were three – each by a freelance writer.

There are a few paid reader-participation spots too – for the committed Christian writer. They pay £5 for any of the following:

- 'What God has done for me' – 300 words plus photograph
- 'A Word in season' – your favourite Bible verse and what it means to you.
- 'Funnily enough' – funny real-life stories, 500 words max.
- 'Dear God' – an honest letter of 300 words.

There is a lively Letters page, 'Your Say', using 9 or 10 letters a week – but no payment is offered for these.

New Christian Herald no longer uses fiction. (Its now long-gone predecessor, *Christian Herald*, ran one short story every week.)

THE NEW WRITER
Incorporating Quartos *and*
Acclaim *magazines*
Editor: Suzanne Ruthven

10 p.a.	£2.95§
Circ: a	Pay: A
NF: 80	F: NIL†
Q: if long	L: NIL
Pay end mth of pubn	

§ subs only £29.50 p.a.
† from subscribers or IStJ short-list
only – see below

The New Writers' Club Ltd
PO Box 60
Cranbrook, Kent TN17 2ZR

Tel: 01580 212626
Fax: 01580 212041

Formed, in 1996, by the amalgamation of *Quartos* and *Acclaim*, *The New Writer* is aimed at ... writers. To qualify that, it tends to be targeted most at those more interested in the creative than the commercial side of writing.

A typical issue of *The New Writer* will contain 48 pages of which fewer than half-a-dozen are taken up by advertisements – and of these, a couple will be for associated publications. (Others tend to be small ads or *'quid pro quo'* adverts for other writing publications.)

On the editorial side there are always four or five 'straight/literary' short stories: these are all either from the Ian St. James Award short list or from subscribers. Stories *from subscribers* are restricted to a maximum length of 2,000 words – any subject, any *genre*. IStJ stories are subject to the rules of the competition (see page 131), i.e., no length limit.

There are few regular columns, as such, in the magazine, but there are a couple of regular spots which are filled by one-off contributors. These are:

- 'Talk Back' – a two-page, around 1,600-word, interview with an interesting writer or publisher.
- 'Vellum' – 1,000-word, one-page articles about the works (rather than the life) of a favourite (literary) author – from Pepys to Steinbeck.

The editor welcomes one-off articles about contemporary writing and publishing policies, etc. She does not want pieces, for example, on how to cope with writer's block and/or the rejection slip. Preferred length is 1,000 words. If you want to offer longer articles (2,000 words max) or mini-series – query first. In one recent issue there were articles about using an old house as the source for several – rather than just one – articles; about using cross-gender names (Alison, Hilary, Pat, etc.) in writing fiction; and one about emotive subjects (which I, at least, found somewhat esoteric). All the articles were rather more 'creative-literary' than hard 'how-to' – but then, the readers of *The New Writer* are perhaps past the need for basic instruction. Decisions on unsolicited articles or ideas come fairly quickly: 4–6 weeks.

The magazine also publishes poetry – any length provided poems are original, structured and interesting, 'offering challenging imagery' – and preferably unpublished. They don't want therapeutic or meandering poems.

19
The bright *stuff*
Editor: Lee Kynaston
Features Editor: Lucy Hunter (Ext. 6320)

M	£1.80
Circ: c	Pay: D
NF: 10	F: NIL
Q: only	L: 60 P
Pay end mth of pub	

IPC Magazines Ltd, SouthBank Publishing Group
Kings Reach Tower, Stamford Street,   Tel: 0171 261 6410
London SE1 9LS   Fax: 0171 261 7634

19 is an IPC magazine directed at young women in their late teens (19-year-olds and younger). The reader of *19* is interested in fashion and beauty ... and boys. And all the other issues that affect young women today.

A typical issue of *19* will consist of around 130 bright, colourful and glossy perfect-bound pages – of which more than a quarter will be advertisements, for perfumes, clothes, cosmetics and other pharmaceutical products. Even driving instruction.

On the editorial side there are several regular sections or departments. Multi-page departments include fashion (everything from trainers to evening wear) and health (which includes the straight-talking – but here, not suggestive or smutty – 'sex files') and beauty. There are other, smaller regular sections/pages including an opinion spot – by a man – and the inevitable astrology column. There is an agony column and a small Letters page: write to '*19*/Your shout'; most letters are back-issue-related, about a hundred words long; and every one gets a prize (e.g., 'a swanky set of make-up').

There are also several one-off features in each issue of *19*. Many of these are written/compiled by the Features Editor herself, or by one of the two staff feature-writers. But a few one-off features have the by-lines of non-staff writers – and are almost certainly commissioned. A few of these one-offs though, could readily be produced by a freelance – given the relevant ideas and experience. And that 'stable' of regular freelances must have started somehow, somewhere. Recent potentially freelance-contributed features have included a 'real life' interview with a rape victim – whose mother had also been raped – and a serious look at how best to produce a job-getting CV. There is even a self-confidence quiz.

The magazine won't look at complete unsolicited manuscripts but is not averse to considering ideas. So ... if you have what you believe is a truly *19*-relevant feature-idea, submit it, in writing, on a single sheet, together with photocopies of, if possible, just one or two similar published features. You *might* then try a phone follow-up about a week later. You *might* get a tentative go-ahead. But if you live up to your 'promise', who knows, you *might* find yourself joining that 'stable' of regulars. (There are a lot of 'mights' there, though.)

NURSERY WORLD

Care and Education in the Early Years
Editor: Liz Roberts
Features Editor: Ruth Thomson

W	£1.15
Circ: a	Pay: C
NF: 70	F: NIL
Q:	L: 300P
Pay end mth of pubn	

Nursery World Ltd
Admiral House, 66–68 East Smithfield,   Tel: 0171 782 3000
London E1 9XY   Fax: 0171 782 3131

Nursery World is a weekly magazine specifically for professional child-carers (nannies, nursery nurses, etc.), teachers and support staff associated with children up to eight years old. It is also of interest to parents – but as a magazine for professionals, it is not in the same mould as the more lay-interest parenting magazines.

A typical issue of *Nursery World* will have 36 saddle-stitched, full colour illustrated pages of which about a dozen will be advertisements. Half the advertisements will be classified ads – for nannies' job vacancies and wanted; display adverts include relevant books, organisations (including trade unions) and local authority job ads.

On the editorial side, there are several regular pages of news and forth-coming events. There is a lively-but-strictly-professional Letters page: the majority of the letters are back-issue-related; each letter gets a small prize. And there are the one-off features.

There will be about half-a-dozen one-off specialist features in most issues of the magazine: several of these will be either staff-produced or too specialised to be within reach of the *general* freelance. There are though, usually one or two features in each issue that could be produced by a free-lance with general experience in the broad child-care profession – which could be said to embrace many mums. But the *slant* of any such feature must be very much from a professional viewpoint rather than that of a parent.

Typical of the potentially freelance features have been: special reports on the effects of poverty on children, children and AIDS, child abduction, whether men should work in nurseries, and whether class size matters; three pages of comments on relating the favourite children's picture-books and standard tales to everyday life; a one-page review of how children might benefit from what's on the Internet; and a two-page report on how to cope with speech impediments. Virtually all features are illustrated, always in colour. Most features include anecdotes and quotes from involved profes-sionals and victims. Most have often quite lengthy, fact-packed sidebars too.

The editor of *Nursery World* is happy to consider brief outlines for *rele-vant* – and correctly slanted – features; decisions come fairly quickly – usually within a couple of weeks.

OPTIONS
Maximum you, minimum fuss
Editor: Helena Jaworski
Features Editor: Ursula Kenny
Editorial Asst: Sarah Lynch (Ext. 6616)

M	£2.10
Circ: c	Pay: D
NF: 20	F: NIL
Q: only	L: 120 P*P
Pay end mth of pubn	

SouthBank Publishing Group, IPC Magazines Ltd
King's Reach Tower, Stamford Street,   Tel: 0171 261 6600
London SE1 9LS   Fax: 0171 261 7344

Options is a glossy, up-market IPC magazine aimed at the modern woman, in the 25- to 35-year age bracket, balancing a job, a home and possibly a family too ... and relatively affluent. (*Options* appears to have moved somewhat more up-market and slightly younger, since last reviewed in the *Handbook*.)

Nowadays, a typical issue of *Options* will have about 140 colourful perfect-bound pages – plus occasional banded supplements – of which about 30 per cent will be advertisements. The advertisements concentrate mainly on cosmetics, pharmaceutical products and foodstuffs – plus the occasional item of clothing or jewellery – and include half a dozen pages of classified ads (offering anything from liposculpture to telephone chat-lines).

Apart from the adverts, there are dozens of pages devoted to the latest fashions (with stockists and prices throughout) and looks – facial and hair-care. Other regular sections include home-making and trendy cooking. Then there are regular pages on astrology, travel ... and the Letters page. There are about a dozen readers' letters in each issue – all back-issue-related, about 100 words each, and with prizes (cosmetic products) for all and for the best.

There are always of course, a number of one-off feature articles too, in each issue of *Options*. Most of these are clearly either staff-written or specially commissioned from a 'stable' of reliable and regular freelances. Some though, could be the result of a writer-initiated outline/query – and the 'stable' regulars must have started up somehow. If you can think of a thoroughly *Options*-relevant feature idea, and ideally have already had work published in other women's magazines, it would be worth submitting a succinct one-page outline. (By post only, and then, maybe after a week or so, try a quick phone-check with the Features Editorial Assistant.) But queries/outlines only – no finished submissions – and really *relevant*.

Recent features that could potentially have been freelance-initiated, have included: a guide to dating in the 90s (about 800 words plus sidebars); advice on 'how to blag your way into the hippest clubs in town' (again, about 800 words plus sidebars); and, for a scientifically inclined freelance, a look ahead to 21st century health advances (about 1,500 words). Each of these features – and many of the others – included quotes from two or three relevant experts.

THE PEOPLE'S FRIEND

The Famous Story Paper for Women
Editor: Sinclair Matheson
Fiction Editor: Margaret McCoy
Features Editor: Hilary Lyall

W	50p
Circ: d	Pay: B
NF: 50	F: 300
Q: NF/F§	L: 600P*P†
Pay on acceptance	

§ query features but not fiction
† plus 300 'snaps'

D. C. Thomson & Co Ltd
80 Kingsway East
Dundee DD4 8SL

Tel: 01382 462276
Fax: 01382 452491

Working to a highly successful formula – plenty of good, entertaining stories – *The People's Friend* has been around since 1869 (before any of us were born) and is still extremely popular. Its readership is women of all ages – from 30 to 80-plus – but perhaps more specifically targeted on the 50-plus.

A typical issue of *The People's Friend* will have about 64 colourful but far from 'brash' pages, of which about a third are advertisements. The adverts, reflecting the readership, are for mail-order clothes, recliner chairs and stair-lifts, decorative plates and other wall-ornaments, and plants for the garden.

On the editorial side, there are always such favourites as knitting patterns, recipes, advice columns on health, gardening and answers to readers' factual queries (*not* an 'agony' column). There is a feature about the beauty-spot pictured on the cover, a collection of readers' snaps and a Letters page. Each week, *The People's Friend* carries about a dozen readers' letters each about 100 words long – each winning a tea-caddy as a prize. (A bigger prize for the best of the week.) Write to 'Letters and Pictures'. Address snaps to 'Snap Happy': they get a fiver each – if wanted back, an s.a.e. is required.

Most issues of the magazine include at least one potentially freelance-contributed feature article – about 1,000 words with a couple of pix seems about right. Topics range from first-person holiday experiences to places from remembered childhood; one that I saw celebrated the last 'practising' British paddle-steamer, the *Waverley*. If you have an idea for a *Friend* article – check with the Features Editor before submitting.

There are one or two poems featured in most issues of the *Friend*. These are all short, 'traditional' (i,e., rhyming and scanning) with a clear meaning or message. Submit just a FEW (six max) at a time, to the Poetry Editor.

But it is for its stories that *The People's Friend* is best known. Apart from a couple of serial episodes there are usually half a dozen short stories in each issue. One, 500–700 words long, is for the kids – nursery/primary age. The other four or five short stories range from a one-page short-short that can be less than 1,000 words, to multi-page stories running up to 4,000 words. Apart from the short-short, the most popular length is about 2,000–3,000 words. Stories can include characters of any age and should be light-hearted and emotional; they should leave the reader with a good feeling. Twist-in-the-tail stories are seldom wanted. Study the magazine before submitting.

Decisions come fairly quickly – about a month. And DCT editors are renowned for their helpful attitude to 'almost there' writers.

PRACTICAL FAMILY HISTORY

Editor-in-Chief: Avril Cross
Editor: Gillian Walden

M	£1.80
Circ: a	Pay: A
NF: 80	F: NIL
Q: no	L: NIL
Pay end mth of pubn	

Armstrong, Boon and Marriott
61 Great Whyte, Ramsey
Huntingdon, Cambs. PE17 1HL

Tel: 01487 814050
Fax: 01487 711361

Practical Family History is a specialist interest magazine and its inclusion in the *Handbook* might therefore be thought inappropriate – but we all have (or have had) families and most of us are at least vaguely interested in our own history. So ... it's included.

Launched in 1997, *Practical Family History* is a sister magazine to the well-established – and very specialist – *Family Tree Magazine*. It is, however, aimed at the lesser experienced, amateur family historian. A typical issue will have 48 saddle-stitched pages illustrated solely in black-and-white; there are only a few pages of advertisements – mostly about ... family tree research.

The magazine has a number of resident experts who contribute various regular columns about family history sources and specific research methods – including, what in another context would be called, an 'agony' column (questions and answers). As well as the resident experts, there are openings for several freelance contributions in each issue.

Typical freelance contributions have included articles on collecting postcards as history sources, re-enacting history in old houses, advice on dating photographs and postcards, the history of child labour in nineteenth-century Derbyshire, and a how-to article on interviewing the elderly to record their memories of days gone by. Most of the articles are either short, half-pagers of about 400–500 words, or one-pagers of 1,000–1,200 words. Most are illustrated – with elderly black-and-white photographs. *Practical Family History* pays on wordage rather than space – and nothing for photographs.

(Don't submit original early photographs – make a photographic copy – not a photocopy – and send that. And beware copyright on old photographs; the magazine reckons 70 years is long enough to be free of copyright. My recommendation would be 100 years: the copyright owner might have been young when the picture was taken – the rule is 70 years after death.)

Unless you are already an expert in family genealogy, don't try offering technical articles – but there is scope for occasional articles along the lines of unusual sources of information, or how you overcame a problem uncovering your own family history. (If you *are* an expert in any aspect of genealogy, you might also be able to write for 'big sister', *The Family Tree Magazine* – which has been going for nearly fifteen years and is read by over 100,000 people, world-wide.)

Decisions on submitted material can take 3 or 4 months at busy times. And be prepared for a long delay after acceptance for publication.

PRACTICAL HOUSEHOLDER
Your Number One Practical Magazine
Editor: John McGowan

M	£2.15
Circ: a	Pay: D
NF: 10	F: NIL
Q: only	L: 80 £*P
Pay end mth of pubn	

Nexus Media Ltd
Nexus House, Azalea Drive
Swanley, Kent BR8 8HY

Tel: 01322 660070
Fax: 01322 667633

The target readership of *Practical Householder* is abundantly clear – the usually male, practical (that lets me out) householder, aged anywhere between 20 and 80, willing and able to do jobs around the house himself (or herself).

A typical issue of *Practical Householder* will have 64 colourful saddle-stitched pages of which about a third will be advertisements. The adverts offer DIY tools and equipment, replacement doors, etc., ready-to-install improvements and various items of household equipment.

The editorial side of the magazine is chock-a-block with photographic and/or drawn, step-by-step illustrations of various DIY activities – from replacing a broken wall-tile to completing a fitted-out bedroom.

Many of the one-off features are freelance-contributed but the writers are usually part of a regular and established 'stable' of proven experts. If, however, you are an expert at some aspect of household improvement work, you might get lucky. Most editors welcome additional competent experts into their existing 'stables'.

There do appear to be occasional opportunities for new writers to provide how-to material: one recent short 'outsider' series explained how to make items of home-office furniture; another dealt with installing home security alarms and lights. All the how-to features have detailed, step-by-step instruction and are profusely illustrated (not necessarily by the writer); they all include sidebars listing suppliers, essential tools, materials needed, etc. Such features go up to about 2,000 words, inclusive of sidebars.

Each issue of *Practical Householder* also includes a number of similar but shorter how-to features: each less than a page, often just step-by-step illustrations plus explanatory captions. These deal mainly with smaller jobs around the house. Offering a picture-script and captions for one of these spots might be a good way of introducing yourself to the editor – but even then, start off with a BRIEF outline/query. Decisions usually come within two to three weeks.

There is also a letters-cum-tips page – write to 'Passing It On' – using half-a-dozen money-saving tips or DIY anecdotes each month. Letters are paraphrased by the editor, the three best get valuable DIY-related prizes, the rest, a tenner.

PRACTICAL PARENTING
From pregnancy to pre-school
Editor-in-Chief: Jayne Marsden
Features Editors: Catherine O'Dolan and
Clare Walters

M	£1.70
Circ: c	Pay: D
NF: 15	F: NIL
Q: only§	L:250£/P*P†
Pay end mth of pubn	

§ No query 'And Finally ...'
† details below

IPC Magazines Ltd
King's Reach Tower, Stamford Street,
London SE1 9LS

Tel: 0171 261 5058
Fax: 0171 261 5366

Practical Parenting is a well-established (launched 1987) IPC monthly magazine for parents with children ranging from 0 to 5 years, and for first-time mums-to-be. A clear and specific target readership.

A typical issue of *Practical Parenting* will have about 130 bright and colourful saddle-stitched pages of which just over 40 per cent are adverts. The advertisements are for medicines and toiletries, food for babies and toddlers, nappies – and lots of good sensible toys for babies and toddlers.

Editorially, there are several regular sections/departments, containing features dealing with pregnancy and birth, child development, baby- and child-care, health, pre-school education, and cooking. There are several pages of giveaways and several of equipment tests – baby cribs to car seats to toys. There are also plenty of opportunities for the new (or about-to-be) mum to write to the magazine. Current openings are:

- Letters (mark envelope 'Letters' – there's a surprise) – 7 or 8 monthly, up to 200 words mostly non-back-issue-related, plus baby-pic (all in colour) – £10 each with a superb prize (worth about £250) for the best.
- 'Happy snaps' – 4 or 5 baby-pix per issue – each winning a batch of videos for toddlers.
- 'Tips' – 4 or 5 30- to 50-word parenting tips each month – attracting a 'goodie-box' of cosmetics for mum.
- 'Meet our Baby' – 4 per month. Answer 4 specific (standard) questions and send a baby-pic. Those published get a £50 Sainsbury's voucher.

There are also, of course, many one-off features in each month's *Practical Parenting*. Most are by experts; some though, could be by 'ordinary' freelance writers with very young children. Recent issues have included features on how a mum recognised meningitis, ideas for things that mum and toddler can make together, and the stages in a baby's growing up. Lengths vary widely but all articles include case-studies (with pix), explanatory sidebars and sources for further advice. If you've an idea for a really relevant *PP* feature, submit a BRIEF outline and hope for a go-ahead.

§ There is one further reader-initiated, back-page spot, entitled 'And Finally ...' Readers' own stories are invited for this page – one I saw recounted an unexpectedly speedy delivery in wildest Africa. It was about 700 words long with a picture of mother and baby. There's no mention of payment in the invitation to 'tell all' – but it would presumably be forthcoming.

PRIMA

Editor: Lindsay Nicholson

M	£1.70
Circ: d	Pay: D
NF: 20	F: NIL
Q: only	L:200£*£†
Pay end mth of pubn	

Gruner + Jahr AG & Co
197 Marsh Wall
London E14 9SG

† details below

Tel: 0171 519 5500

Prima is a very practical magazine – full of lots of things to make and do. It is aimed at women of all ages – but the 'core' readership is probably those in the 25 to 50 age bracket. And, broadly speaking, it's not a great market for the 'ordinary' freelance.

A typical issue of *Prima* will have about 160 bright and colourful saddle-stitched pages – of which a good third will be advertisements. The adverts – for foodstuffs, clothes, cosmetics and pharmaceutical products, among other things – bear out the target reader-age suggested above. Its practicality too is borne out, not only by the editorial sections/departments, but also by the paper sewing pattern that is always bound into the magazine. (There is usually a knitting pattern too, in the editorial pages.)

Editorially, the colourful pages include major sections on fashion, beauty-care and cooking (a dozen or so pages in each section). Other regular features cover health, home decoration, the 'usual' agony column and 'stars' page, gardening advice – and a large 'crozzle' (a form of cross-word puzzle). There's a regular travel spot too – usually several small 'info-bites'.

There are two straightforward 'reader-participation' opportunities in *Prima*:

- Letters – write to 'You Tell Us' – 6 or 7 100-word back-issue-related letters per month – earning £25 each and £50 for the best.
- Tips – write to 'Prima Tips' – 8 or 9 30- to 50-word hints (with photograph if possible) - earning £25 each.

Women writers who make up any of *Prima*'s patterns can also send (non-returnable) photographs of the finished product to 'Look What We Made'. They use half-a-dozen pix each month paying £25 each, £50 for the best.

Opportunities for freelance writers to contribute one-off features to *Prima* are few – but if you hear of anyone (check your local papers) with an interesting real-life story, the editor might be interested in your working it up. One such story told of a tug-of-love mother; another was about the problems of jury service. There is also a regular back page 'Last laugh' feature – one I saw was about 30 snippets under the heading, 'You know you're not so young when ...'. If you've got an idea for something like this, it might get slotted in. Study what they've used recently, and then query the editor – but don't hold your breath. If you put up a really *Prima*-relevant idea, they may get back to you; if the idea's not right, they probably won't.

READER'S DIGEST
The world's favourite magazine
Editor-in-Chief: Russell Twisk

M	£1.90
Circ: e†	Pay: D
NF: NIL	F: NIL
Q: n/a	L: 600 § £
Pay end mth of pubn	

† 27 million copies in 48 editions
worldwide
§ not letters – anecdotes and quotes

11 Westferry Circus, Canary Wharf
London E14 4HE

Tel: 0171 715 8000
Fax: 0171 715 8716

Reader's Digest is not a potential market for 'ordinary' freelance writers. That is not to say that they do not commission work from professional free-lances – they do, but it's a very tough market. It is though, a marvellous market – and encourages submissions – for anecdotes, quotes and jokes.

A typical issue of *Reader's Digest* will consist of nearly 200 A5-sized perfect-bound pages of which about 30 per cent will be advertisements – from exotic holidays to stairlifts, medicines to investment opportunities, cars to packaged food – reflecting the universal nature of the readership. Editorially, there are about twenty one-off features and a condensed non-fiction book. But, as above, these are of little interest – other than as a reader – to the 'ordinary' freelance writer.

Of far greater interest are the well-paid anecdote/joke/filler/quote items:

● 'Life's Like That' – true, unpublished personal experience stories, revealing human nature and humorous or appealing incidents from everyday life – the Editor likes about 300 words, in letter form, which can be edited down to about 100 words. They pay £200 each.
● 'All in a Day's Work' – true unpublished stories about humour in the workplace – same length, same pay.
● 'Studied Wit' – as above, but humour at college.
● 'Humour in Uniform' – as above, but in the armed services.
● 'Laughter, the Best Medicine' – jokes, your own or (first report accepted) heard on radio or TV or seen in print. £125 each – about 100 words.
● 'Quotable Quotes', 'Ways of the World', 'Personal Glimpses', 'Points to Ponder', 'Towards More Picturesque Speech' – interesting or amusing short anecdotes, quips or quotes – seldom more than 100 words. They pay £60 each.

Send contributions – including your name, address, and daytime tele-phone number on each sheet – for any of the above, marked EXCERPTS. Published material should also include source, date and page number. *Reader's Digest* neither acknowledge nor return any such submissions and decisions can take several months. They don't notify rejections but pay (well) on acceptance: do not, therefore, offer the same material elsewhere for about six months.

A revised booklet, *Writing for Reader's Digest*, is available: £5, by post.

SAGA MAGAZINE

Editor: Paul Bach

M	£1.50 §
Circ: e	Pay: D
NF: 35	F: NIL
Q: only	L: 300 £*£
Pay end mth of pubn	

§ subs only, £12.95 p.a.

Saga Publishing Ltd
The Saga Building, Middelburg Square,
Folkestone, Kent CT20 1AZ

Tel: 01303 711523
Fax: 01303 712699

Saga Magazine is the magazine of the Saga Club, which is closely associated with Saga Holidays and other companies within the Saga Group. (Saga offer a wide range of other services nowadays, from insurance and health-care to credit cards and investment advice.)

A typical issue of *Saga Magazine* has 160-plus pages of which about 50 per cent are advertisements. The adverts range from electric-powered mobile chairs to garden kneelers to mail-order clothes – and many of the wide range of Saga services. Within the advert element of the magazine there are also always details of various Saga holidays on offer. Saga offers its services exclusively to those over 50 – the magazine is aimed at *lively*, active, and relatively affluent people of both sexes within that age group.

The magazine has many regular sections or columns: there are opinion columns from Keith Waterhouse and Clement Freud, among others; there are pages on gardening, motoring, finance and home economics and many other topics; there is a 'Can I Help You' column by Katherine Whitehorn; and a lively Letters section. More than two dozen letters are featured in each issue of *Saga Magazine* – they pay £50 for the month's best, £10 for the rest. A good market for letter-writers.

In addition to the regular features, there are always a number of one-off articles. These are mostly profiles-cum-interviews with interesting people within the 'Saga age group'; they run to 1,200–1,800 words, with colour illustrations usually magazine-provided or -arranged. A typical issue of the magazine would have 15 or more such articles. Recent subjects have included Twiggy, Christopher Lee, ex-King Constantine of Greece ... and the Tamworth Two (the now-pardoned pig escapologists, for those who've been out of the country for the last few years).

The snag – from a freelance viewpoint – is that many of these features are either staff-written or commissioned from regulars.

However, some are undoubtedly provided by out-of-the-blue freelances – maybe two or three per issue. If you have adequate writing experience and know someone of 50-plus, with a really interesting story, send in a detailed outline to the editor – and cross your fingers. Don't submit anything on spec. And expect a response to an editorial query within three or four weeks – you could get a *tentative* go-ahead.

THE SCOTS MAGAZINE
The World's Top-Selling
Scottish-Interest Title
Editor: John Methven

M	£1.20
Circ: b	Pay: A
NF: 120	F: 10
Q: no	L: 140 –
Pay on acceptance†	

† words only: pix paid later

D. C. Thomson & Co Ltd
Albert Square
Dundee DD1 9QJ

Tel: 01382 223131
Fax: 01382 322214

The Scots Magazine – which was first published in 1739 – is a magazine for Scotland. (In that respect it is similar to *Country Quest* with its coverage of Wales and the Borders – see page 31.) The target readership of *The Scots Magazine* is obvious – Scots, worldwide, of both sexes and of all ages but leaning towards the more mature. You don't have to be a Scot to write for it – although judging by many of the contributors' names, I guess it helps – you just have to write about Scotland and things Scottish.

A typical issue of *The Scots Magazine* will have about 112 perfect-bound A5 pages with lots of colour. About 30 pages will be taken up by advertisements – for hotels and holiday accommodation in Scotland, for Scottish ephemera (including such services as ancestor research), for tourist-geared shops, for new homes in Scotland, and for Scottish-based charities.

On the editorial side there are a number of regular sections: Scotland-related book and music reviews, news of what's on in Scotland, comments on the origins of Scottish words, an illustrated poem ... and a thriving but non-paying Letters page – longish letters, mainly back-issue-related. There are several sections of attractive colour photographs (picture-postcard-like) – and many freelance-supplied one-off features.

Editorial guidelines suggest that articles can be any length within the range 1,000 to 3,000 words – as long as everything is Scotland-related. Nearly all features are illustrated – more in high-quality colour than in black-and-white.

Recent one-off features have included a 2,500-word, 4 colour pix, personal experience story about learning to pan for gold (Scottish, of course); a black-and-white illustrated (3 pix) article of about the same length giving the history of Scottish tollhouses; and just 700 words plus a spectacular 5-page set of colour pix on the delights of Harris, in the Hebrides. There was an amusing 1,800-word (artist-illustrated) personal experience article ... about the problems of being a writer in a Scottish family – and nearly 3,000 nostalgic words plus 4 black-and-white pix about cycling in the Scottish mountains (before the days of mountain bikes).

There is often a short story in *The Scots Magazine* too – same length restrictions, often humorous, always very Scots ... and sprinkled with dialect. The magazine usually adds witty line drawings to stories.

Editorial decisions – no preliminary queries necessary, just make sure whatever you submit is Scotland-related – come quickly, within days.

SHE
For women who know what they want
Editor: Alison Pylkkanen
Features Assistant: Amanda Kelly

M	£2.10
Circ: c	**Pay: D**
NF: 10§	**F: NIL**
Q: only	**L: 70 *P**
Pay end mth of pubn	

§ NIL unsolicited

National Magazine House
72 Broadwick Street,
London W1V 2BP

Tel: 0171 439 5000
Fax: 0171 439 5350

She is an up-market magazine for young women in the 25-45 age bracket: affluent, stylish, probably working (certainly with a full life), an enthusiastic home-maker, probably with young kids – and very interested in their sensuality.

A typical issue of *She* will have about 200 glossy, perfect-bound pages of which almost a half can be advertisements – for cosmetics, fashions, kids clothes and medication, foodstuffs and household equipment. Editorially, there are regular sections covering fashion and beauty, living and food (including some mouth-watering recipes) and parenthood. There are columns covering personal health, entertainment, books, travel, relationships and astrology. And a Letters page – half-a-dozen letters a month, nearly all back-issue-related and with a prize for each month's best. There are also, of course, several one-off features in each issue of *She*. BUT ...

She's editorial policy is crystal clear (although printed in the smallest possible typeface on the masthead page):

They will not consider unsolicited material at all – nor will they return anything submitted.

Against that, they don't write all the features in house; some are from freelances, usually from their 'stable' of known and reliable writers. But that 'stable' must have started somehow, somewhen, somewhere. So ... if you have what you think is a particularly *She*-relevant idea, you can always try sending them a BRIEF written outline/query (plus just one or two photocopies of similar work published in a similar magazine). If they like the outline, they'll get back to you fairly quickly; if not, not at all. After three or four weeks you might try phoning the Editorial Assistant for a reaction – but don't build your hopes up. And whatever you do, study the magazine carefully before putting up an idea.

Typical one-off *She* features have recently included a discussion of how management styles can be based on kids' books – Alice, Pooh, the Famous Five, etc.; a review of unacceptable behaviour (e.g., snogging in public) and a discussion on whether sex was better in the 50s, 60s, 70s, 80s, or 90s.

Always worth a real hard try – great magazine, good payers. They're ... *women who know what they want.*

TAKE A BREAK
Magazine of the year
Editor: John Dale
Fiction Editor: Norah McGrath

W	60p
Circ: e	Pay: D
NF: NIL§	F: 50
Q: N/A	L: 1500£*£†
Pay end mth of pubn	

§ many True Life stories
† details below

H. Bauer Publishing
25–27 Camden Road
London NW1 9LL

Tel: 0171 284 0909
Fax: 0171 284 3778

A cheerful tabloid-style magazine aimed primarily at women readers but clearly picking up more than a few men too, *Take a Break* has repeatedly been chosen Magazine of the Year. It is rather like its sisters and competitors, *that's life!* and *Chat* – its core readership is women of around 30 but it is of interest to all ages.

A typical issue of *TaB* (as it frequently refers to itself) has around 64 pages of which about 20 per cent are advertisements – for mail-order catalogues, household necessities and food. On the editorial side, there are several regular sections, dealing with fashion, food, health, etc. There is also the almost inevitable astrology feature and several 'problem' pages. There are many reader-participation competitions in each issue of the magazine – with prizes ranging from £1000 in cash, or a free holiday, to a small car.

Like most other magazines in similar mould, *TaB* always has a number of True Life features – about a dozen per issue. (Where do all the amazing stories come from? Answer, of course, people's amazing lives.) These range from the 5 or 6 two-page stories (earning £250 each) to the 'My Operation' 500-word half-pagers (earning £75 each). Amazingly, there is even a 'Pet true confession' spot (earning £100). Be warned though, these really are true life stories, with photographs – unlike the purely fictional 'Confessions' of years gone by (on which many of today's writers cut their teeth).

Take a Break is a good market for short-short stories – in their 'Coffee Break' slot. These stories are straight – i.e., they don't have to be romantic or 'twisters' – and 1,000 words maximum. Occasionally, there are two such stories in an issue.

TaB is also a good opportunity for those who write hints, tips and Letters – and for 'happy snappers'. Regular spots include:

- 'Oh happy days' – cheerful snaps, about 15 per issue, earning £50 each.
- 'Readers' Brainwaves' – 15+ tips, many illustrated, about 30 to 50 words each, earning £20 – or £50 if illustrated.
- 'Boot sale tales' – half-a-dozen each week, 50-100 words plus picture, earning £30 a time.
- 'Letters' – about 10 a week, 50-100 words long, earning £25 for the best, £20 for the rest, plus £25 per photograph.

The magazine likes a daytime phone number with all letters, hints, etc.

that's life!

Editor: Janice Turner
Fiction Editor: Emma Fabian

W	49p
Circ: ?	Pay: D
NF: NIL§	F: 50
Q: N/A	L: 2500£*£†
Pay on acceptance	

§ many True Life stories
† details below

H. Bauer Publishing
2nd Floor, 1–5 Maple Place,
London W1P 5FX

Tel: 0171 462 4700
Fax: 0171 636 1824

A bright and breezy women's magazine from the Bauer stable, *that's life!* is aimed at a broad cross-section, from teenagers to grannies – but more directly at the 20–35-year-old woman. A typical issue will consist of 48 colourful pages of which no more than about half-a-dozen will be advertisements – mostly for mail-order catalogues and the like.

Living up to its title, *that's life!* always feature a lot of the universally popular true life stories: five or six one-and-a-half-page 1000-word stories, a two-page spread of three or four 'It happened to me' 500-worders and one-page 'My secret' or 'Kids are us!' one-offs. They pay £250 for the one-and-a-half-page stories and £150 each for the others. A major warning though: these really are true stories and include photographs of the people involved. Unless you lead a complex and lurid life, not much scope for the ordinary freelance writer.

As well as the personal experience stories, *that's life!* has a number of regular (usually two-page) features: fashion, health, beautycare, cooking, home decoration and furnishing, readers' problems ... and, of course, an astrology column. The magazine also features a considerable number of competitions – word searches, crosswords and space-fillers – all good for reader-participation.

There is also a well-paid regular one-page 1,000-word 'twist-in-the-tail' short-short story. (They're paying £300 each!)

It is, though, for its letters and 'fillers' spots that *that's life!* is particularly attractive to the 'ordinary' freelance. It's best to study these carefully before submitting – they specify the need for originality and exclusivity. There are regular spots (numbers per week based on sampled issues only – these will obviously vary) for:

- 'Aren't men daft' – 50–100 words, 8 items, £25 each (£50 for the best).
- 'The things they (kids) say' – 50 words, 2 items, £25 each.
- 'Tightwad tips' – 30–50 words, 16 hints, £15 each plus £20 for picture (£40 for best – including photograph).
- 'Rude jokes' – lengths vary, 5 jokes, £15 each.
- 'Letters' (most not past-issue-related) – 30–50 words, 12 letters, £20 each (£25 for the best) plus £5 each for photographs.

In all, one of the biggest letter/filler markets – and a good payer, both for these and for the short-short story.

THE THIRD ALTERNATIVE

The magazine of extraordinary *new fiction*
Editor: Andy Cox

Q	£3.00
Circ: a	Pay: A
NF: 12	F: 28
Q: F no, NF yes L: 10 –
Pay end mth of pubn

TTA Press
5 Martin's Lane, Witcham,
Ely, Cambs CB6 2LB

Tel: 01353 777931
Fax: 01353 777931

The Third Alternative is one of Britain's most original magazines; it publishes 'an exciting mix of extraordinary new fiction, stunning artwork and provocative comment'. Now supported financially by the Eastern Arts Board, it is a fine example of how a small, independent press magazine can grow into the publishing mainstream – without sacrificing its principles. It publishes modern, character-led horror, fantasy and SF ... and borderline, 'between-genre' material – they call it 'slipstream'. Its readership is young(ish) – and international.

A typical issue of *The Third Alternative* will have 60 much-illustrated, glossy, saddle-stitched pages – the internal pages are illustrated in black-and-white, the cover, in colour. There are only four pages of advertisements – from mainstream (HarperCollins) and other publishers, and the like.

Editorially, the magazine carries half-a-dozen regular columns – including commentary from Britain, and from the US – and a small (unpaid, back-issue-related) letters section. The bulk of the magazine is taken up with short stories and articles.

The short stories are, as already intimated, 'new wave' and largely within – or not too far removed from (i.e., 'slipstream') – the horror, fantasy and SF genres. They are often by well-known or up-and-coming authors – and sometimes by first-timers. Maximum story length is a not-too-rigorous 8,000 words – the shortest story in one recent issue was almost 5,000 words long. (No 'short-shorts' here.) The stories themselves can best be described – other than 'new wave' or 'modern' – as uninhibited. In their field, the stories are excellent – and in the past have won many prestigious awards and been reprinted in relevant anthologies. Submit just one *relevant* story at a time, unsolicited (plus s.a.e., of course). Post flat or one fold only.

On the non-fiction side, *The Third Alternative* regularly publishes profiles of 'relevant' authors: John Fowles and Christopher Priest ... but not Jeffrey Archer or Catherine Cookson. These interview-based profiles discuss the career of the writer overall and cast a critical eye over their work. They also use essay-type articles reviewing some aspect of a well-known author's work. Influential film-makers too can be profiled or their work looked at. These articles are generally 2,000–3,000 words long and illustrations are particularly welcome. Ideas for other articles – comment, humour, etc. – are welcomed. For all *relevant* non-fiction though, query first with a brief outline.

Whatever you do though, study the magazine before submitting anything – *Woman's Weekly* it ain't.

THIS ENGLAND
Britain's Loveliest Magazine
Editor (of both): Roy Faiers

Q	£3.50
Circ: c	Pay: A
NF: 80	F: NIL
Q: no	L: 100+ –
Pay end mth of pubn	

and

EVERGREEN

Editor (of both): Roy Faiers

Q	£2.75
Circ: b	Pay: A
NF: 80	F: NIL
Q: no	L: 100+ –
Pay end mth of pubn	

PO Box 52, Cheltenham
Gloucestershire GL50 1YQ

Tel: 01242 577775
Fax: 01242 222034

This England is a glossy quarterly, founded in 1968, devoted to the glories of the English heritage. It is strong on nostalgia and beautiful, but always traditional, things. (A picture of an old stone bridge, for instance, would almost certainly – and understandably – be more acceptable than one of a slim modern reinforced concrete one.) It uses a lot of pictures, mostly nowadays in colour, with black-and-white pictures mainly of historical origin. The target readership of *This England* is middle-aged or older, of both sexes and probably reasonably affluent and well-educated.

A typical issue of *This England* will consist of 80-plus lavishly illustrated perfect-bound pages of which – as publishing policy, '... advertisements should provide a service to readers rather than dominate the magazine.' – no more than about half-a-dozen will be advertisements. The advertisements are either classified small ads for everything from vanity book publishers to holiday accommodation, or display advertisements mainly for the magazine's other products, publications, etc.

Editorially, the typical issue of *This England* will contain a number of features forming parts of continuing series such as English country churches, the 'hymn villages' of England, England's shire counties, English surnames, and English heroes. There are also two regular long-standing sections of the magazine which offer good opportunities for the freelance writer: notably 'Cornucopia' and 'Forget Me Nots'.

'Cornucopia' uses a dozen or more short (up-to-date) pieces per issue, each about 300 words and usually colour illustrated: recent topics have included a 60-feet high milestone, a full-sized working replica of Captain Cook's ship *Endeavour*, a well in Carshalton, Surrey, named after Anne Boleyn, and a best-selling photograph of Isambard Kingdom Brunel.

There are two or three 'Forget Me Nots' in each issue; these are longer pieces, 600–800 words each and pure nostalgia – 'When I was six, my family ...' Such pieces are sometimes illustrated by the staff artist, and sometimes with old black-and-white photographs.

There are also many opportunities for longer one-off feature articles in *This England*. Typical of such features are a profile of a wartime hero, a look at the home-town of TV's *Last of the Summer Wine*, a collection of 40 strange facts about ... [a county], and an essay about an afternoon in the country. Such features should not normally exceed 2,000 words and are usually much-illustrated – in colour.

This England also uses quite a lot of poetry, often as page-end fillers. The Editor says that short poems – about a dozen lines long – stand the best chance and that poems should be meaningful rather than 'clever'. The poems are noticeably traditional in form too, invariably having metre and rhyme. Don't submit more than three poems at a time.

If you are a writer-photographer, *This England* offers even more opportunities: they use a lot of free-standing pictures – almost all, now, in colour – either as two-page spreads or as captioned snippets. The big spreads are mainly out-door scenes and preferably include one or more persons *doing* something; the smaller pix are often of an interesting building, statue or 'thing'. Colour pix must be transparencies and the Editor prefers them to be 2¼ inches square (120 film) or larger. When black-and-white prints are appropriate, captions and the photographer's name and address should be on the back.

Editorial rejections can be quick – in about a month. Decisions on marginal material often take considerably longer – up to three months. The Editor particularly advises writers NOT to enquire about the fate of their submissions in less than three months. He says, 'Material is invariably returned without further consideration to an over-zealous contributor.' Ouch! Contributors are also cautioned to submit seasonal material at least five months before the appropriate publication date – and invite editorial attention to the relevance of the date.

There is also a sister publication, *Evergreen*. This is a pocket-sized quarterly of about 150 perfect-bound pages produced by the same editorial team; its needs and policies too are much the same as those of *This England* – but it uses material relevant to Scotland and Wales *as well as England*.

Like *This England*, *Evergreen* welcomes unsolicited submissions about people and places, about crafts, traditions and beauty-spots, about towns and villages; and all similarly old-fashioned, nostalgic and reflective. All the above comments about *This England* are equally relevant to *Evergreen*. All material submitted for *This England* is automatically considered for possible use in *Evergreen* – and vice versa.

And remember – don't chase the Editor in less than three months (and even then, only very 'gently'). If you do, your work is rejected.

TV QUICK

Editor: Lori Miles

W	60p
Circ: d	Pay: D
NF: 10	F: NIL
Q: only	L: 700£*£†
Pay end mth of pubn	

† see below

H. Bauer Publishing
25-27 Camden Road
London NW1 9LL

Tel: 0171 284 0909
Fax: 0171 284 0593

With so many – including free – sources of TV listings, any magazine of listings has to offer more than just details of what's on. *TV Quick* does just that: it offers a variety of celebrity news and gossip, readers' real life stories and many of the features of more conventional magazines. The readership of the magazine is inevitably broad but leans somewhat towards women in their twenties to forties, with young-to-teenage children.

A typical issue of *TV Quick* will contain about 68 colourful saddle-stitched pages. Of these, there may be a dozen pages of advertisements – for mail-order clothes and catalogues, decorative plates and similar wall ornaments, food and ... ciggies. There will of course also be thirty-odd pages of detailed TV (and less-detailed radio) programme listings – with recommendations of what to watch. There's also a regular £1,000-prize crossword.

Editorially, there are regular pages on health, finance, cooking and shopping, plus an agony column run by Molly Parkin and an astrology column from Russell Grant. There are several pages of news and gossip about the TV and pop scene including a new celebrity question-and-answer feature. And there are several Real Life readers' stories – they pay £200 a time for these. (They really are true stories and include photographs of the 'storyteller', so there are only very limited freelance opportunities here.) There are also one or two interview articles about TV personalities: if you know someone in the TV (performing) business, it's worth checking whether *TV Quick* would be interested in a feature article. But always check first.

Of more likely relevance to most 'ordinary' freelance writers, *TV Quick* has a lively Letters and Tips page. Details:

- Letters – write to 'Quick Line' – 7 or 8 letters a week, about 50–100 words each, non-back-issue-related, £25 for the best, £10 for the rest.
- Tips – write to 'Quick Tips' – 7 or 8 modern tips each week, about 20-30 words each, £10 each. (One typical recent tip suggested tying two knots in a washing line – to keep the prop in place on windy days.)

TV Quick does not use any fiction.

TWINKLE

Editor: Bill Moodie

W	60p
Circ: ?	Pay: A
NF: NIL	F: 300 §
Q: yes	L: 300 P †
Pay on acceptance	

§ details below
† for very young girls only

D. C. Thomson & Co Ltd
Albert Square
Dundee DD1 9QJ

Tel: 01382 223131
Fax: 01382 322214

Twinkle has one of the youngest target readerships of any magazine in Britain: little girls of four to nine years old. And it has been hitting that target for thirty-plus years. Recently it has undergone a slight face-lift – the pages are now somewhat bolder in their colours – but the formula for the basic content remains much the same.

A typical issue of *Twinkle* will have 24 colourful saddle-stitched pages with no advertisements at all. It will contain five or six picture-stories and two or three much-illustrated text stories. There will also be a several pages of puzzles, competitions etc., reproductions of readers' art-work, and letters and snaps from some of the 'older' (eights and nines) readers – who all get a prize.

The picture-stories in *Twinkle* are for young children; they differ some-what from those for older readers. There are no speech-balloons, thoughts or sound-effects within the frames or panels (the individual pictures): all the text, including speech, is in a 20- to 30-word caption beneath the picture. The pictures (when 'read' by child) and the captions (when read by mum) will each stand alone ... and work together (child on lap, looking at pix, Mum reading).

The picture-stories in *Twinkle* are about long-standing characters – the copyright in which is owned by the publishers. Anyone may offer scripts using the characters – but only to *Twinkle*. Regular characters/story-series include: Nurse Nancy (6–8 frames, 2 pages – Nancy works in a dolls' hospital); Goody Gumdrops (a newish character, 6-8 frames, 2 pages – Goodie lives in Sweetie town where everyone is named after a sweet); Silly Milly (6 frames, 1 page – Milly's always in a muddle); My Baby Brother (3–4 frames with captions in 4-line verse, 1 page – 'I' is a little girl); Patch (6 frames, 1 page – Patch is an adventurous kitten).

Text stories vary from one-page, under 200 word 'Toyroom Tales' to four-page stories of around 400–500 words. In all such stories the text is very simple and easy-to-read: sentences average less than ten words, para-graphs seldom exceed twenty words, lots of dialogue. You need to study several issue of the magazine to get a 'feel' for the type of stories they want.

For both picture-script and text stories it is best to enquire first for specific requirements – not all characters are available for contributed scripts and story requirements change. Remember – the writer doesn't have to do the drawings, only describe them. (See page 118.) And D. C. Thomson are well-known for their encouragement of promising writers.

THE WEEKLY NEWS

Editor: David Hishmurgh

W	45p
Circ: c	Pay: B
NF: 10	F: NIL
Q: no	L: 1000£*£†
Pay on acceptance	

† details below

D. C. Thomson & Co Ltd
Albert Square
Dundee DD1 9QJ

Tel: 01382 223131
Fax: 01382 201390

The Weekly News is a tabloid-sized weekly newspaper aimed at the TV-quiz-game and Coronation Street viewer – which covers a multitude. The target readership is somewhat down-market – but, despite the regular sports pages, more women than men.

A typical issue of *The Weekly News* will have 30-plus pages – all 'newspaper-style' (headlines, cross-heads, etc.). Spread out within the pages there will be the equivalent of about 4 pages of advertisements – for mail-order goods, UK holiday resorts, health products ... and other DCT publications. Editorially, there are several pages of news – including keeping up-to-date with the 'soap' scene – and a number of regular columns. The regulars include 'best buys', health and life-style, a page of puzzles and jokes, gardening, DIY, and sports.

Most issues of *The Weekly News* feature one or two 'readers' own stories' told in the first person – but not necessarily by the actual protagonist. The paper welcomes such stories – up to 2,000 words. They are also interested in celebrity interviews/profiles – and not necessarily only of top stars. Readers' stories and celebrity profiles apart, there's not a lot of scope for the 'ordinary' freelance writer – except for cartoons, jokes, puzzles and the obvious fillers, letters and tips.

These latter opportunities are:

- 'In the Bag' – the letters page. They use about a dozen 'original and exclusive' letters each week – not usually back-issue-related, often amusing/embarrassing, about 100 words long. £10 for the best, nothing for the rest.
- 'Marriage Lines' – frequently, petty embarrassments. They use 3 or 4 per week, each 30–50 words long. £10 for the best, £5 for the rest.
- 'Top Tips' – any area (cooking, gardening, etc). They use 7 or 8 per issue, each 30–50 words long. Again, £10 for the best, £5 for the rest.

All letters, tips, etc. should be addressed by title (above) to *The Weekly News*, 144 Port Dundas Road, Glasgow G4 0HZ. (And remember, these are meant to be from readers, not from 'writers' – see page 121.)

WOMAN

Editor: Carole Russell

W	60p
Circ: e	Pay: D
NF: 20§	F: 50
Q: only	L: 600 £*£
Pay end mth of pubn	

§ see below

IPC Magazines Ltd
King's Reach Tower, Stamford Street
London SE1 9LS

Tel: 0171 261 5000
Fax: 0171 261 5997

Woman has been around since 1937 and is still going strong. It is a bright and breezy weekly designed to be a 'good, quick read'. Its target readership is all 'mid-market' (i.e., not short of a bob or two but not seriously affluent) women, from teenagers to grannies – but its core readership has to be those in the 25–40 age bracket.

A typical issue of *Woman* will have 60 colourful saddle-stitched pages of which over a dozen will be advertisements – for a range of products from food to cosmetics, from pharmaceutical products to mobile phones. There are also usually a number of special reader offers.

Editorially, there are a number of regular sections: fashion, beautycare, health, and cookery. There are several pages of news about the soaps and other celebrities. There is an astrology column and several problem-answer pages. Like so many other magazines, there are several real life stories in each week's issue – *Woman* offers up to £250 for such stories.

The magazine carries a one-page short-short story each week. Study published stories carefully before submitting.

They also use the occasional freelance feature from 'ordinary' writers. If you have previously had features published in similar magazines and happened to hear of a really interesting woman's experience or way of life, you might try querying the editor. (In one recent issue there was an interview with a woman who married an Arab and now lives in a Bedouin tent. Another feature investigated the results of cosmetic surgery – that one had to have been pre-commissioned, but it conveys an idea of the sort of feature used.) But don't hold your breath – and don't send any original documents.

There is a lively Letters page in *Woman* (write to 'You Tell Us') using about a dozen short (50–100 words) letters each week. Letters earn £5 each plus £5 for associated pix, and the best of the week gets £25.

WOMAN ALIVE
for today's Christian woman
Editor: Liz Proctor

M	£1.80
Circ: a	Pay: B
NF: 60	F: NIL
Q: prefer	L: 70 –
Pay end mth of pubn	

Herald House Ltd
96 Dominion Road
Worthing, West Sussex BN14 8JP

Tel: 01903 821082
Fax: 01903 821081

Woman Alive is Britain's only Christian magazine aimed at women. It covers all denominations and deals with issues relevant to active Christians as well as general interest features – celebrity profiles, cookery, fashion, etc. It is aimed at women of all ages – married, single, divorced or widowed – but particularly the 25–45 age group. It is a very readable magazine: although Christian values and beliefs are apparent on every page, it does not *inappropriately* preach. Unless you are a committed Christian though, there is little point in submitting material or ideas: the editor asks for a brief biography – Christian (and writing) background – from all new writers. (She also asks for samples of published work – but if you have none, try anyway.)

A typical issue of *Woman Alive* will consist of 48 saddle-stitched pages (about 50 per cent in colour) of which about a third are advertisements – for religious books, diaries and holidays, for charities, and for jobs.

On the editorial side there are regular (commissioned or staff-written) features on contemporary issues, on health, and on Bible reading; there are book reviews and a round-up of religious news. There is a Letters page – 'Viewpoints' – using half-a-dozen back-issue-related letters ... but no pay.

There are also several one-off freelance-contributed features – some, like the 1,300-word celebrity interviews, are usually commissioned, others are 'writer-initiated'. The magazine welcomes submissions (but it would be wise to get your idea agreed first) for these regular slots:

- 'A life in the day of ...' – a *first person* account of a well-known Christian woman's daily life – 800 words. (A recent one was about a language signer at church.)
- 'Testimony' – a *first person* account of how the writer became a Christian – 800 words.
- 'Travel/Leisure' – a 750–1,200 word, conventional travel/holiday article written from a Christian perspective. (One was about a Bible week under canvas.) Good colour photographs are essential – offer at least 3 or 4 – they reimburse film/processing costs rather than paying per picture.
- 'Practical/craft' – a step-by-step, well-illustrated How-to article, with sidebars listing materials needed, contact addresses, etc. (Recently, there was advice on setting up a barter trade group.) Length should be in the range 750 to 1,200 words and again, pix are welcomed. Similar articles are welcomed dealing with homes, gardens or cookery – on a budget.

WOMAN & HOME

Editor: Jan Henderson
Fiction Editor: Belinda Hollyer
Features Editor: Sam Murphy (Ms)
(Ext. 5144)

M	£1.80
Circ: d	Pay: D
NF: 28§	F: 12§
Q: only	L: 60 *P
Pay on acceptance	

§ NIL unsolicited

IPC Magazines Ltd
King's Reach Tower, Stamford Street,
London SE1 9LS

Tel: 0171 261 5176
Fax: 0171 261 7346

Woman & Home is an up-market monthly magazine from IPC; it is aimed at women of 40-plus, relatively affluent, intelligent, pleasantly house-proud and in a stable family relationship. They may or may not be working women.

A typical issue of *Woman & Home* will have about 160 much-illustrated perfect-bound pages – of which nearly a third will be advertisements. The adverts are mainly for clothes, cosmetic and pharmaceutical products, holidays (cruises and the like) and 'interesting' foodstuffs.

Within the editorial pages, each issue of *Woman & Home* will have regular sections/departments covering homes and gardens, fashion and beauty, health, cooking, and travel. There are regular pages offering give-aways, telling readers' star 'fortunes' and offering advice ... and crossword puzzles. There is a small, non-paying Letters page, using mostly back-issue-related letters and giving one prize to the best letter of the month.

There are several one-off features and a short story in every issue of the magazine. But ... in small print in the masthead, they say:

We never accept unsolicited manuscripts or pictures, including fiction, and if submitted, we cannot return them.

So ... don't send them anything on spec. And certainly don't bother them at all (see below), if you're not already well-experienced.

But some of the one-off material in the magazine is undoubtedly free-lance-supplied. I noticed a few features recently that could – potentially – have been writer-initiated and then commissioned from freelance writers. They were: a feature on second marriages (1600 words plus two 450-word case studies and a factual sidebar); a comparison of NHS and private medical facilities (2,000 words, 2 mini case studies, and a sidebar); and an 1,100-word travel article (plus sidebar) about Florida. And even their 'stable' of well-proven reliable freelances had to start somewhere.

If you have a really *relevant* idea for a *Woman & Home* feature, send them a BRIEF outline, by post, plus just one or two photocopied sheets of similar published work. If the idea grabs them, they'll get back to you – if not, they won't. If – and only if – you're a well-published, fairly 'literary', and/or well-known, short story writer, and not yet on *Woman & Home*'s 'list' it might be worth asking whether you can send them a story or two.

WOMAN'S JOURNAL

Editor: Marcelle d'Argy Smith
Features Editor: ???

M	£2.20
Circ: c	Pay: D
NF: 20	F: NIL
Q: only	L: 80 *P
Pay end mth of pubn	

IPC Magazines Ltd
King's Reach Tower, Stamford Street,   Tel: 0171 261 6622
London SE1 9LS   Fax: 0171 261 7061

Woman's Journal is a glossy, up-market IPC magazine for comfortably-off women aged 30-plus. It is for women *as women*, rather than as wives, mothers, home-makers or even career women – although they could be all of these things.

A typical issue of *Woman's Journal* will have 160-plus glossy, perfect-bound pages, of which more than 40 per cent will be advertisements. Supporting the 'women as women' attitude, the largest number of adverts are for clothes and fashion accessories but there are also a lot for perfumes, cosmetics, food, etc.

Within the editorial side of the magazine there are a number of regular sections: the most important – at least in number of pages, around 25 per issue (and again supporting the 'women as women' attitude) – is fashion, illustrating both designer and high street clothes. There are also large sections of the magazine devoted to beauty, health and food.

As well as the major sections of the magazine, there are also several regular columns: 'You don't have to ...' a column by Michael Bywater, taking a wry look at life; travel pages (you could ask about writing a travel piece – but don't hold your breath), astrology and a Letters page. (Half-a-dozen, 200-word, usually back-issue-related letters, the best each month receiving a really good gold-plated fountain pen: write to Sarah Ogborn, 'Open Line' Editor, at Room 1538, *Woman's Journal*.)

As well as the regular sections, the magazine usually carries about eight to ten one-off features in each issue. Most of these are clearly staff-initiated, commissioned work. But there appear to be one or two such features in most issues that are, or could be, writer-initiated work. In one issue there were features about why men love 'glossy' women, and how more and more women are now stepmothers – and the problems they face. (There was also a delightful short feature, '50 ways to tell if you're still young' – almost certainly staff-written – but it could have been an outside idea. Whoever wrote it, it worked for me! As long as you didn't have to notch up all 50.)

If you have an idea for a *Woman's Journal*-relevant feature, send them a BRIEF outline, by post, along with just one or two photocopies of similar published work – and hope for a positive response. You might try phoning after a week or ten days – to check. But don't go ahead without approval – and don't submit completed manuscripts on spec.

WOMAN'S OWN

Editor: Terry Tavner (Ms)
Features Editor: Melanie Whitehouse
(Ext. 7009)

W	60p
Circ: e	Pay: D
NF: NIL §F: NIL §	
Q: only	L: 450£*£
Pay end mth of pubn	

§ see below

IPC Magazines Ltd
King's Reach Tower, Stamford Street
London SE1 9LS

Tel: 0171 261 5474
Fax: 0171 261 5346

Woman's Own is the sister magazine of IPC's *Woman* (see page 75) and is similarly bright and cheerful. Like *Woman*, its target readership is all 'mid-market' women, from teenagers to grannies, but its core readership is perhaps slightly older – say 30- to 45-year-olds.

A typical issue of *Woman's Own* will have 60 colourful saddle-stitched pages of which about a dozen are advertisements – mainly for food, home-making goods, and cosmetic and pharmaceutical products. There are also a number of special reader offers – one was for a heat massage mat.

On the editorial side there are several regular sections: fashion, health, beautycare, cooking, home-making, money and travel. There is an astrology column and several problem-answer pages – and several real-life stories. There is no suggestion in the magazine that *Woman's Own* is eager to receive such stories (compare with, say, *that's life!* see page 68, which offers good money for true stories) or pay for them but presumably they do.

There are no obvious opportunities for 'ordinary' freelance article-writers; recent one-off features have dealt with male prostitutes/escorts, what women think about stopping smoking, and how Ruby Wax got herself a husband (by padding out her bra). Nor does *Woman's Own* welcome feature material out of the blue – see below.

There is a regular short-short story spot, 'Take five' – but once again, the magazine does not welcome submissions.

In small print on an inside page the magazine states, 'We regret that we cannot ... answer any letters or return submitted material unless accompanied by an SAE. We also regret that we cannot accept unsolicited fiction manuscripts.' That's quite clear, and fair enough. But if you have already had material – features or short fiction – published in similar magazines, and have an idea for a really *relevant* article or story, it might be worth querying the editor. Make it just a short query letter and send only photo-copies of previously published work, plus an s.a.e. – you might not get them back, nor even a reply. Don't hold your breath.

Among the regular columns there is, of course, a Letters page. This uses half-a-dozen or more letters each week, often as long as 100 words, about half 'back-issue-related' and earning £5 each and £25 for the best. They also offer £10 for the 'Snap of the week' and £15 for a short 'It makes me mad' spot (letter plus pic). Photographs are non-returnable.

WOMAN'S REALM

Editor: Kathy Watson
Fiction Editor: Sally Sheringham
Features Editor: Sally Morgan

W	57p
Circ: d	Pay: D
NF: NIL§	F: NIL§
Q: only	L: 800£*£†
Pay end mth of pubn	

§ NIL unsolicited
† details below

IPC Magazines Ltd
King's Reach Tower, Stamford Street,
London SE1 9LS

Tel: 0171 261 6033
Fax: 0171 261 5326

Woman's Realm is designed to appeal to a wide range of readers; its prime readership – as evidenced by advertisement and editorial pages – is a married/partnered woman in her mid to late thirties, probably with children, possibly in part-time employment, and without a lot of 'spare' money. But it is clear that *Woman's Realm* also has many younger and older readers.

A typical issue of *Woman's Realm* will have 60 colourful saddle-stitched pages of which about a fifth are advertisements – for food, ornaments, health products, etc. And there are always several pages of product news – kitchen and other household items – and readers offers and give-aways.

On the editorial side there are a number of cheerful features – ranging from Real Life stories to comparisons of how a group of readers reacted to a common situation. There are regular sections/pages dealing with health, cookery, gardening, fashion, beautycare, knitting, and travel. There are smaller columns dealing with money, the law, and astrology.

Although conceivably at least the travel articles could be freelance supplied, the magazine does not welcome unsolicited articles – and is unlikely to return any submitted. (They don't even return the snapshots submitted to the Letters page.)

There are a couple of short stories in each issue of *Woman's Realm*. One is a two-pager (up to 2,400 words) and the other a one-page, possibly twist-in-the-tail, short-short. As with features, the magazine does not welcome unsolicited short stories – and may not return anything they receive.

Despite the discouragement, the features and stories in *Woman's Realm* are not all staff-written; much is supplied by freelance writers known to them to 'deliver'. If you have a really relevant feature or story idea and have had similar work published elsewhere – in a similar populist magazine – it would be worth sending a BRIEF letter to the relevant department-editor enclosing *photocopies* of one or two published pieces. You might get a reply (or get your name onto their list of possibles for the future) – but don't hold your breath. Basically, they don't want new blood – until you surprise them.

Woman's Realm is though, a good spot for Readers Letters – 'From You to Us': they use about a dozen letters or tips per issue, paying £5 each – £25 for the best letter. They even use an occasional poem. They pay £25 for a one-a-week 'Snap Happy' and £15 for a 'Baby of the Week' snap. Another participation spot is 'Moments to Cherish' – 100 words and a photograph – earning £25. (Address to 'Moments', Features Dept.)

WOMAN'S WEEKLY

Editor: Gilly Sinclair
Fiction Editor: Gaynor Davies

W	54p
Circ: e	Pay: D
NF: 50	F: 150
Q: wise	L: 700£*P†
Pay end mth of pubn	

† details below

IPC Magazines Ltd
King's Reach Tower, Stamford Street
London SE1 9LS

Tel: 0171 261 5000
Fax: 0171 261 6322

Woman's Weekly was first published in 1911 and is still going strong. But it has modernised itself. It is no longer the purple-covered journal of 'royalty, romance and recipes' (the old, well-tried formula), although there are still lots of good recipes and fiction. The readership of *Woman's Weekly* nowadays is a broader church – but with the emphasis slightly on the more mature woman of 35-plus years.

A typical issue of the magazine will have about 68 colourful saddle-stitched pages of which just over 20 per cent will be advertisements – for clothes, flowers, food, ornaments and the like. On the editorial side there are many regular sections: always several pages of scrumptious-sounding recipes, and a similar sized section containing a knitting or other pattern. There are regular pages covering gardening, travel, fashion, health, home-craft and parenthood; and of course, there are astrology and 'agony' columns. In common with many of its competitors, *Woman's Weekly* now includes at least one Real Life story per issue – as always, not of great interest to the freelance writer – they really are true stories.

There are one-off feature articles too but it would be unwise to submit anything on spec – query your idea first; most of the opportunities seem to be 'celebrity-associated' or maybe about a special garden.

The *Woman's Weekly* Letters page is a good opening for writers that way inclined; they use a dozen or so letters (more or less any length, 30–200 words), paying £10 each plus a special gift for the best of the week. Write to 'Lovely to Hear From You'. They use the occasional 'top tip' too (£10, same address) and have a weekly spot for an amusing snap (£15, sent to 'Snapped').

But it is for its fiction that writers (and readers, of course) are most interested in *Woman's Weekly*. There is always a serial – possibly by the likes of Catherine Cookson) – and two or three short stories in each issue. 'Your Coffee Break Read' – for which 'twist-in-the-tail' submissions are particularly welcome – is a short-short of about 1,000 words (currently earning £230). One I read was only slightly 'twisty' – about the problems of being a house-husband.

The other stories are of any length from 1,000 to 3,000 words, have believable, *up-to-date* characters, an unpredictable storyline, an element of tension or conflict and, possibly, but not necessarily, an element of romance. I enjoyed reading one about a young-looking woman coming to terms with the surprise news of imminent grandmotherhood.

WRITERS' FORUM
Britain's most complete 'How to Write'
magazine
Editor: Morgan Kenney
Deputy Editor: Anthony Donnelly

Q	£3.75 §
Circ: a	Pay: A
NF: 80	F: NIL†
Q: prefer	L: NIL
Pay end mth of pubn	

§ subs only, £14.50 p.a.
† from comps only

21 Belle Vue Street
Filey, North Yorks YO14 9HU

Tel: 01723 513279
Fax: 01723 513279

Founded in 1993, the quarterly *Writers' Forum* has had a variety of publishers and editors but now seems to have 'settled down' with Morgan Kenney as Publisher and Editor. It is a 'reader-friendly' small-press magazine.

A typical current issue of *Writers' Forum* has 64 saddle-stitched pages (including the cover). Of these, about 10 pages are advertisements – for writers' services (manuscript appraisals, plot suggestions, etc.), writing courses, other small press magazines, and printers offering self-publishing services. Most readers of *Writers' Forum* are enthusiastic learners rather than experienced writers. The magazine lives up to its sub-title promise: it offers a lot of what such readers want – detailed how-to advice. It also features the occasional personal experience tale, illustrating that all have similar problems.

Each issue of *Writers' Forum* contains some 20+ articles, about three-quarters of which are 'how-to's, some within short, 4- or 5-part series. Recent short series have included Research for Novelists by fellow Allison & Busby author, Jean Saunders, and Marion Field on her successful self-publishing experiences. One-off articles have included well-known poet (and another prolific fellow Allison & Busby author) Alison Chisholm on organising your writing time, Sally Zigmond on writing style and Stuart Drinkwater on murder methods (for crime-writers, not for protagonists).

As well as the one-off articles and 'how-to' series, there are a number of other regular sections in the magazine. These include: news of poetry and short story competitions (including *WF*'s own regular ones – and, of course, the prestigious annual Petra Kenney Poetry competition, see page 131), news from writers' circles, reviews of writing books, and a crossword. An 'agony column' has just been started – writers', rather than 'personal' problems, of course. There is usually one feature on photography – often by Hugh Graham, a practical freelance photographer of no small expertise – and a decidedly worthwhile market study section. (I found a really good, totally new-to-me market a year or so ago from one of *WF*'s market reports.)

The editor welcomes feedback correspondence and the Letters page has recently been reinstated – but no pay/prizes.

Don't waste editorial time offering poetry or fiction, except for their competitions. Decisions are sometimes less-than-instant – it's a small crew – but it's a good magazine to deal with. It's worth supporting.

WRITERS' MONTHLY
Incorporating The Writer
Managing Editor: Alan Lewis

M	£2.75§
Circ: a	Pay: C
NF: 120	F: NIL†
Q: prefer	L: 60 *P
Pay 2 mth after pubn	

§ subscription only, 33 p.a.
† from comps only

Market Link Publishing plc, The Mill,
Bearwalden Business Park, Wendens Ambo,
Saffron Walden, Essex CB11 4JX

Tel: 01799 544200
Fax: 01799 544201

The publishers, since 1985, of *Writers' Monthly* went into voluntary liquidation in early 1997. After a four-month break, the magazine was relaunched in September 1997 under the aegis of Market Link Publishing Ltd – who also publish some dozen or so other specialist magazines. The relaunched *WM* is brighter, brisker and is already attracting more advertisements than its predecessor. It is available on subscription only.

A typical issue of the new *Writers' Monthly* contains about 36 saddle-stitched pages of which around 7 pages will be advertisements – for things like competitions, home-study courses and writers' services. There are black-and-white illustrations – either artwork or photographs – on virtually every page. And the articles are getting shorter. The target readership is obvious – writers. To qualify that bald statement, most readers will be near, or have achieved publication, some will be expert writers in their own field seeking broader interests. You can't 'write down' to them.

Regular columns include: a detailed and up-to-date market study review of several related-subject magazines (use it to keep this *Handbook* updated); a 'writer's pilgrimage' look at the home territory of a famous author; a 'Newsline' feature; a profile of a current big name author; a technology page; a blossoming Letters page (4 or 5 letters per issue with a £10 book token for each month's best. Send letters to the Editor at Taunton.) – and a joint 'problems and ideas' page by yours truly. (And no doubt there will be other regular features to come.)

As well as the regular features, *Writers' Monthly* has plenty of freelance-supplied one-off articles and short series. Recently, the series have included travel-writing, romance-writing and – again from me – a 'course' for absolute beginners. One-offs have included advice on how to get the settings right in your fiction; how to use the occasional foreign phrase in your writing – for atmosphere; how to write and sell jokes to cartoonists; and on interviewing techniques. All from experts in their field. They also welcome some humour.

Generally speaking, one-page articles (1,100 words max, 1,000 better) are the most popular but the editor also uses a number of shorter, half- and two-thirds-page length. Preliminary outlines are preferred to finished articles – even for the shorter ones. And, bearing in mind the readership, if you aspire to write for *Writers' Monthly* – you must know your stuff.

STOP PRESS: Publication suspended.

WRITERS NEWS

Editor: Richard Bell

M	£2.40§
Circ: a	Pay: B
NF: 5	F: NIL†
Q: wise	L: 60 *P
Pay end mth of pubn	

§ notional single-copy price
subscription, £43.90 p.a. – includes
Writing Magazine
† from comps only

Writers News Ltd
P. O. Box 4
Nairn IV12 4HU

Tel: 01667 454441
Fax: 01667 454401

Writers News was founded in 1989, by David St. John Thomas, and it has gone from strength to strength. It fosters the concept that readers (on subscription only) are *members* of a club. It also emphasises the news element of its title: each issue contains a dozen or so pages of news items.

Subscribers to *Writers News* also receive – included in the subscription (see above) – each year's six bi-monthly issues of *Writing Magazine* (see page 85). In the months when *Writing Magazine* appears, *Writers News* contains around 28 pages – about 50 per cent news, 20 per cent advertisements, and the rest, a few of the regular columns. Nearly all the expected regulars and features are in *Writing Magazine* those months.

In the alternate months, when it's 'on its own', *Writers News* has 50+ pages. Of these, a dozen or so are news, a similar number are filled with adverts ... and there are lots of regular columns/pages/sections – including a lively Letters Page which gives a £10 book voucher for the monthly Star Letter. The other regulars include a 2- to 3-page interview with a leading author, an excellent 2- to 3-page market review (of batches of related-subject magazines), sections on children's books, technology, writing style, writing practice, and a couple of chatty columns – one by the publisher and one from the editorial side. There are regular poetry 'workshops', critical reviews of the magazine's prize-winning short stories, and a problems page.

Listing the regulars exemplifies the overall 'shape' or 'feel' of the magazine – there are very few one-off articles by other than the regular writers. (That doesn't necessarily mean that if you have an idea for a one-off article or short series, *Writers News* wouldn't be interested in seeing it. Just that such one-offs are few and far between.) All features – regular columns, series or one-offs – are by experts; this is no place to 'break your duck'.

The target readership of *Writers News* is, of course, all writers – and any writer will find much of interest in it. But it tends to aim more at the struggling beginner than at the successful writer. Its editorial attitude tends to encourage – in my view, perhaps over-enthusiastically – the idea of self-publishing; although it of course comes down hard against vanity publishing.

Decisions tend to come quickly – in less than a month – and outlines are preferred to complete articles. *Writers News* also welcomes news items – including 'your own news', so don't be bashful.

WRITING MAGAZINE
The Voice of Writing
Editor: Richard Bell

2M	£2.50§
Circ: a	Pay: B
NF: 10	F: NIL†
Q: wise	L: 30 *P
Pay end mth of pubn	

§ free to Writers News subscribers
(see page 84)
† from comps. only

Writers News Ltd
PO Box 4,
Nairn IV12 4HU

Tel: 01667 454441
Fax: 01667 454401

Launched in 1992 as a quarterly news-stand partner to the by then well established *Writers News* (see page 84), *Writing Magazine* is supplied free to *Writers News* subscribers. Now a bi-monthly, each issue contains all the regular columns that would otherwise have been in that month's issue of *Writers News* – plus several more.

A typical issue of *Writing Magazine* will contain about 64 pages of which almost a quarter are advertisements: for *Writers News'* correspondence courses and book club, for tuition and conferences, for writing services – particularly offers of manuscript-vetting by experienced author-editors – and for printers, etc. offering to assist those intent on self-publishing. The rest of the magazine consists very largely of regular columns/pages/sections.

Regular features in *Writing Magazine* include an excellent 3-page interview (by Judith Spelman) of a famous author plus up to half-a-dozen shorter, one-page unattributed profiles of lesser authors. There are columns and series dealing with research, legal matters, finance matters, fitness, information technology (computers including, still, the much-loved old Amstrad PCW), photojournalism, screen-writing, poetry, article-writing, various aspects of fiction-writing and writing for children. There is a beginners' column, a page or so of book reviews, a readers' problems page and a Letters page. (About half a dozen letters per issue, the best attracting a book token prize.) You name it, there's probably a regular column about it.

Other than an excellent market study article in each issue, there is virtually no writing *news* in *Writing Magazine* – it's all in the associated *Writers News*. The magazine itself always contains one or more writing competitions of its own. The target reader of *Writing Magazine* is slightly harder to define than that of *Writers News* ; clearly all readers are potential writers, but perhaps because of its news-stand 'casualness', slightly less dedicated than *News* 'members'. Like *Writers News* though, the magazine is clearly aimed at the wannabe rather than the more experienced writer.

There are few opportunities for one-off articles by non-regular contributors – but it is possible for an experienced and knowledgeable writer to break in with ideas for one-off articles or short series. One-page articles need to be around 800 words, with longer articles running to a maximum of about 1,500 words. The best initial approach is with an outline. Decisions come quickly – less than a month. But *Writing Magazine* is no place for breaking your publication duck. If you aren't an expert, don't waste the editor's time.

YOURS
– for the young-at-heart
Editor-in-Chief: Neil Patrick
Executive Deputy Editor: June Weatherall

M	80p
Circ: c	Pay: A
NF: 120	F: 12
Q: no	L: 600£*£
Pay end mth of pubn	

YOURS Editorial
EMAP Choice Publications Ltd
Apex House, Oundle Road,
Peterborough PE2 9NP

Tel: 01733 555123
Fax: 01733 312025

YOURS is produced in association with Help the Aged; it is aimed at lively senior citizens. It is clear from the magazine contents – adverts, questions, friend-tracing, etc. – that its target readership is pensioners, of both sexes, but nearer their seventieth than their sixtieth birthdays.

A typical issue of *YOURS* consists of about 150 saddle-stitched pages, of which almost half (about 45%) are advertisements. Many of the adverts are for such age-giveaways as recliner and motor-powered chairs, retirement homes, investment opportunities, stair-lifts and mail-order support footwear.

The magazine abounds in regular features. There are columns on gardening, legal matters, social benefits, beautycare, pets, money matters and health. There are recipes for meals for one or two, patterns for knitting and embroidery, and a problem-solving page. There are reports on older people's lives from around the country (by a 'regular'); there is a chatty column by comedian Roy Hudd; and there is always a short story. This can be up to 1,700 words long (but is often shorter); at least some – but not all – of the characters are usually senior citizens. This is a good freelance market – but there's lots of competition and usually a stack of accepted stories awaiting publication.

As well as the regular features, there are a number of openings for one-off freelance articles. These are usually 700–800-word one-page features, often nostalgia-based; recent topics have included the loss of a loved pet, coping with noisy neighbours, memories of a famous walker of the 60s, and a series of personal love stories. There is also usually a travel article. The same qualification as applied to the short story, above, is equally applicable to features – they are welcomed but will often be put 'on hold' for quite a while before publication. Don't query in advance – submit completed articles.

YOURS is also particularly attractive for its Letters page. This uses up to 50 short (and sometimes abbreviated) letters and tips per issue. The pay is small, £3 each and a tenner plus a pen for the best – but it's a big 'market'. If you also send a photograph relevant to the letter, it probably enhances your chances of publication. There is also a 'Soapbox' feature – readers' views on selected topics – but there's no mention of payment for this.

There are also *YOURS Special*s – bumper extra issues, four times a year – which also use letters, short stories and articles.

2

The 'Best' Markets

Any assessment of the 'best' market for freelance writers is inevitably subjective. Every writer has a favourite magazine, often the one that most readily accepts that writer's work. Certainly, I have my own favourites – and not necessarily the ones at the top of the list that follows. Despite its subjective nature though, there does seem to be some value – and interest – in this ranking process; it is therefore retained.

The ranking process has been kept as simple as possible in order that it be easily understood. The alphabetical payment groups – which are derived from payment rates – are converted into numerical marks for use as multipliers. The probable annual total of freelance contributions, both non-fiction and fiction (itself a subjective assessment), is then multiplied by the payment mark to give a ranking figure.

For convenience, the payment groups are repeated here, with the relevant numerical mark alongside:

Payment £ per 1,000 words	Payment group	Payment mark
£1 to £40	A	1
£41 to £60	B	2
£61 to £100	C	3
Over £100	D	4

As an example, selecting *Heritage* at random, its payment group is C, taken as a mark of 3; its likely intake of writer-initiated freelance material for a year has been assessed at about 20 articles. A mark of 3 times an intake of 20, gives an overall ranking figure of 60 – which is where it appears in the following table. Similarly, *The People's Friend*, taking 50 articles and 300 short stories per year, totalling 350, and a payment group of B (converted into a mark of 2), gets an overall ranking figure of 2 x 350 = 700 – which puts it high in the list of 'best' markets.

There are changes in the rankings of some magazines since the last edition of the *Handbook*. These are mostly due to my reassessment of the magazine's freelance intake which, hopefully, reflects the inevitable changes in editorial policies over time. Nevertheless, many 'old favourites' – *The Lady*, *Woman's Weekly* and *Bella* – are still there, at or near the top of the list.

THE BEST MARKETS

Rank	Magazine	Total intake (F + NF)	Payment group = mark	Total mark (Intake x pay)
1	*The Lady*	320	C = 3	960
2	*Woman's Weekly*	200	D = 4	800
3	*The People's Friend*	350	B = 2	700
4	*New Christian Herald*	300	B = 2	600
5	*Bella*	100	D = 4	400
	My Weekly	200	B = 2	400
7	*Writers' Monthly*	120	C = 3	360
8	*Home & Country*	100	C = 3	300
	Twinkle	300	A = 1	300
10	*Candis*	72	D = 4	290
11	*Woman*	70	D = 4	280
12	*The Countryman*	130	B = 2	260
13	*Choice*	60	D = 4	240
14	*Active Life*	76	C = 3	230
15	*Nursery World*	70	C = 3	210
16	*Best of British*	200	A = 1	200
	Bunty	200	A = 1	200
	Good Housekeeping	50	D = 4	200
	Take a Break	50	D = 4	200
	That's life!	50	D = 4	200
21	*Business Opportunity World*	60	C = 3	180
	Country Quest	180	A = 1	180
	Goldlife	45	D = 4	180
	Home Run	60	C = 3	180
25	*Cat World*	170	A = 1	170
26	*The Field*	40	D = 4	160
	Woman & Home	40	D = 4	160
	Amateur Gardening	50	C = 3	150
	Best	50	C = 3	150
30	*Homes & Gardens*	35	D = 4	140
	Saga Magazine	35	D = 4	140
32	*Yours*	132	A = 1	132
33	*The Scots Magazine*	130	A = 1	130
34	*The Big Issue*	30	D = 4	120
	Brownie	60	B = 2	120
	Country	40	C = 3	120
	Essentials	30	D = 4	120
	Mizz	40	C = 3	120
	Woman Alive	60	B = 2	120
40	*Chat*	50	B = 2	100
	Family Circle	25	D = 4	100
	Geographical	25	D = 4	100

THE BEST MARKETS (continued)

Rank	Magazine	Total intake (F + NF)	Payment group = mark	Total mark (Intake x pay)
	Kids Alive!	100	A = 1	100
	More!	25	D = 4	100
45	Foreword	45	B = 2	90
46	Country Life	20	D = 4	80
	Evergreen	80	A = 1	80
	The New Writer	80	A = 1	80
	Options	20	D = 4	80
	Practical Family History	80	A = 1	80
	Prima	20	D = 4	80
	This England	80	A = 1	80
	Woman's Journal	20	D = 4	80
	Writers' Forum	80	A = 1	80
55	Interzone	75	A = 1	75
56	Heritage	20	C = 3	60
	Ideal Home	15	D = 4	60
	Amateur Photographer	20	C = 3	60
	Practical Parenting	15	D = 4	60
60	Dogs Monthly	40	A = 1	40
	Illustrated London News	10	D = 4	40
	Mother & Baby	10	D = 4	40
	19	10	D = 4	40
	Practical Householder	10	D = 4	40
	She	10	D = 4	40
	The Third Alternative	40	A = 1	40
	TV Quick	10	D = 4	40
68	The Weekly News	10	B = 2	20
	Writing Magazine	10	B = 2	20
70	Writers News	5	B = 2	10
71	Reader's Digest	0	D = 4	0
	Woman's Own	0	D = 4	0
	Woman's Realm	0	D = 4	0

3

Who Uses What?

It is of course not possible to list, in any precise manner, the stories and articles that will attract the interest of an editor. Editors are always looking for something new – but not too new – something that they haven't done before and that they think will particularly interest their readers. It is one of the tasks of the freelance writer to come up with new ideas that will spark off the Editor's interest. Having said that, there are broad categories of article subjects which fall naturally into the areas of interest of different magazines.

The lists below, broad though the subjects may be, offer a general idea of which magazine is most likely to be interested in articles on which subject.

Similarly, short stories intended for readers in a certain age bracket are often best written around characters of a broadly similar age. It is therefore possible to suggest that a story about teenage love is best suited for one group of magazines – and unlikely to sell to a magazine with a readership aged generally in their late forties. The story market lists categorise magazines generally by age groups but also by those magazines interested in the increasingly popular 'short-short' story – complete in less than, say, 1,400 words (and often much less).

ARTICLES – BY SUBJECT

General interest/factual/biography

Active Life
Best of British
The Big Issue
Candis
Cat World
Choice
Country
Country Life
The Countryman
Country Quest
Evergreen
The Field
Geographical
Goldlife
Good Housekeeping
Heritage
Home & Country
Homes & Gardens
Illustrated London News
The Lady
The People's Friend
Practical Family History
The Scots Magazine
This England
Woman's Journal
Yours

Animals/nature study

Cat World
Country
Country Life
The Countryman
Dogs Monthly

Evergreen
Home & Country
The Lady
This England

The national heritage/nostalgia – the countryside and the buildings

Best of British
Country
Country Life
The Countryman
Country Quest
Evergreen
The Field
Good Housekeeping
Heritage

Home & Country
Homes & Gardens
Illustrated London News
The Lady
The People's Friend
Saga Magazine
The Scots Magazine
This England

'How-to' and 'Things to do' features

Amateur Gardening
Amateur Photographer
Business Opportunity World
Cat World
Chat
Choice
Dogs Monthly
Essentials
Family Circle
Foreword
Goldlife
Home Run
Homes & Gardens
Ideal Home

More!
Mother & Baby
My Weekly
19
Nursery World
Practical Family History
Practical Householder
Practical Parenting
Prima
The New Writer
Writers' Forum
Writers' Monthly
Writers News
Writing Magazine

Family matters – advice on relationships, children, etc.

Bella
Choice
Family Circle
Mother & Baby
New Christian Herald
19
Nursery World

Options
Practical Parenting
She
Woman Alive
Woman and Home
Woman's Journal

'The mating game'

Mizz
More!
19

Options
She

Personality profiles/interviews

Active Life
Best of British
The Big Issue
Business Opportunity World
Candis
Cat World
Choice
Country
Goldlife
Good Housekeeping
Homes & Gardens
Illustrated London News
Interzone
My Weekly
New Christian Herald
The New Writer

19
Options
Saga Magazine
She
The Third Alternative
TV Quick
The Weekly News
Woman Alive
Woman and Home
Woman's Journal
Woman's Realm
Woman's Weekly
Writers' Monthly
Writers News
Writing Magazine

Business/financial matters

Business Opportunity World
Choice
Essentials
Homes and Gardens

Home Run
Ideal Home
Woman and Home

Travel

Active Life
Goldlife
Home & Country

The Lady
Prima

Real life/personal experiences

Active Life
Bella
Best
Cat World
Chat
Choice
Family Circle
Goldlife
Good Housekeeping
The Lady
More!
Mother & Baby
My Weekly
New Christian Herald

Nursery World
Options
Practical Parenting
Prima
Saga Magazine
Take a Break
That's life!
TV Quick
The Weekly News
Woman Alive
Woman's Weekly
Writers' Forum
Yours

Articles for young children

Brownie

Kids Alive!

FICTION

**Short-short stories
– for young children**
Brownie
Candis
Kids Alive!
The People's Friend
Twinkle

**Picture-story scripts
– for young children**
Bunty
Kids Alive!
Twinkle

**Short stories (1,400-plus words)
– for women, over 30 years old**
Active Life
Bella
Candis
The Lady
My Weekly
The People's Friend
Woman and Home
Woman's Weekly

– for both sexes, all ages
Active Life
The People's Friend
The Scots Magazine
Yours
And the 'Literary' and 'Small'
magazines (see Chapters 4 and 5
– pages 94–96 and 97–106)

– for women, under 30 years old
Bella
My Weekly

**– for all, for SF/fantasy/horror
stories**
Interzone
The Third Alternative

**Short-short stories (single-page, up to about 1,400 words max) – for
women, various ages**
Active Life (both sexes)
Bella
Best
Chat
More!
My Weekly

Take a Break
That's life!
Woman
Woman and Home
Woman's Weekly
Yours (both sexes)

Serials
My Weekly
The People's Friend
Woman and Home
Woman's Weekly

Poetry
Best of British
The Countryman
Evergreen
The People's Friend
The Scots Magazine
This England
And the 'Literary' and 'Small'
magazines (see Chapters 4 and
5 – pages 94–96 and 97–106).

4

Literary Magazines

The publications reviewed in Chapter 1 include many markets for short stories. But these are largely restricted to the women's magazines, whose requirements are usually (but not exclusively) for stories with a romantic flavour. There is not a large market in the more popular magazines for 'straight' short stories. But there are still the literary magazines; fewer than there were, often paying very little, but all welcoming good short stories for *paid publication*. Most of them publish poetry too – and some even pay for it.

The literary magazines are usually produced by a single enthusiast, or by a small like-minded group, working in their spare time for the love of literature. Almost inevitably, the magazines are produced on a very small budget; it is therefore even more important than usual to enclose a stamped self-addressed envelope, and be prepared to wait for a reply. Remember to put your name and address on everything submitted too. And DO study a copy of the relevant magazine before submitting to it. They are all different.

There is but a fine line dividing the literary magazines from some that I have classified as Small Press Magazines. Several small press magazines are decidedly literary, well produced and long established, with significant circulations. Poets and writers of non-mainstream fiction are advised to peruse the next chapter with equal care. In future editions, there may need to be some reshuffling of categories.

The more interesting of the literary magazines are:

Ambit (1959) Quarterly £6.00 per copy incl p&p (£22 per annum)
Editor: Dr Martin Bax
17 Priory Gardens, London N6 5QY

Uses a dozen or so short stories per year which can be up to 10,000 words long. Publishes 300–400 poems per year. A decision on submitted work can take up to three months. Payment is likely to be about £5 per page and is made on publication; two copies of the issue of the magazine containing a contributor's work are always provided.

London Magazine (1954) Bi-monthly £5.95 per copy (£28.50 per annum)
Editor: Alan Ross
30 Thurloe Place, London SW7 2HQ

Uses about 20 short stories each year, including six in each of two regular short story issues, with a preferred length of 2,000–5,000 words.

Also publishes about 200 poems each year plus occasional memoirs, and articles on art, photography, theatre and film. Decisions on submitted work are given quickly, usually within a week. Payment for short stories and articles is around £15 to £25 per 1,000 words; for poems the payment is at £20 per page; for both, on publication. A copy of the issue of *London Magazine* in which a contributor's work appears, is always provided.

Orbis (1968) Quarterly £3.95 per copy
Editor: Mike Shields
27 Valley View, Primrose, Jarrow, Tyne and Wear NE32 5QT

Basically a poetry magazine, *Orbis* nevertheless uses a few of what the editor prefers to call 'prose pieces' (i.e., not formula fiction) each year – but no longer than 1,000 words each. Publishes up to 200 poems per year. Decisions often by return of post – but never take longer than two months. Unlike some other literary magazines, *Orbis* receives no grant aid from anywhere, so that payment for stories and poems is a nominal £5 'per acceptance' – which can be more than one piece of work.

Payment is on acceptance and one copy of the relevant issue is always provided. (Two more free copies can be supplied in lieu of payment – on request.) See also page 131 for details of *Orbis*'s Rhyme International Competition.

Stand Magazine (1952) Quarterly £3.95 per copy incl p&p (£11.95 per annum)
Editors: Lorna Tracy and Rodney Pybus
179 Wingrove Road, Newcastle-on-Tyne NE4 9DA

Unashamedly left of centre, *Stand Magazine* uses 15–20 short stories each year (maximum length, 6,000 words). The magazine also uses about 70 poems per year. Decisions on submitted work are usually given within a month. Payment rates are £25 per 1,000 words for fiction and £25 per poem or per page for longer verse; payment is made on publication; a copy of the relevant issue of *Stand Magazine* is also provided.

For many years, the magazine has been running a biennial short story competition – see page 131: the next competition, starting in January 1999 closes June the same year. (The next one is expected to start in January 2001 and close the following June.) A similarly biennial poetry competition has now also been introduced (details on page 132): it opened January 1998 and closed June 1998. (The next one will therefore presumably run from January to June 2000.)

World Wide Writers (1998) Quarterly £5.99 per copy incl p&p (£20 per annum, UK; $60, airmail US) Cheques payable to Writers Workshop.
Editor: Alex Keegan   Publisher: John Jenkins
PO Box 3229, Bournemouth BH1 1ZS

A 250-page perfect-bound quarterly magazine, *World Wide Writers* has filled in the gap left by the demise of *Raconteur* – which was, itself, aimed at readers deprived of *Argosy*. And it is truly international.

WWW operates in much the same fashion as did *Raconteur*: it does not accept unsolicited fiction as such – virtually all of its short stories come from its ongoing quarterly competitions. (One or two are specially commissioned from 'names'.) A typical issue of *WWW* contains about 20 short stories, a number of poems (also via a competition) and the occasional 'essay'.

Rules for the short story competitions are simple: the work must not have been previously published, can be in any genre, between 2,000 and 5,000 words, *literate* rather than *literary*, *readable* and entertaining. They must, of course, be typed, double-spaced, big margins, etc. – or on disk (ASCII or Word), or by e-mail (to writintl@globalnet.co.uk). Entries must be accompanied by an entry form (in magazine, or a leaflet – send s.a.e. – or on Internet) and a £6 entry/reading fee. Competitions close at the end of January, April, August and October – if you miss a closing date, the entry is automatically moved forward to the next quarter's competition (no entries are held for more than three months). All entries receive a grid-based critical feedback with brief notes. For a further £4 you get a full one-page crit. In each issue/quarterly competition, prizes range from £125 to £625, all plus publication in *WWW*. There is a further prize of £3,125 plus a Waterford Crystal bowl for the year's best story.

The quarterly poetry competition requires unpublished poems of no longer than 80 lines, typed, double-spaced plus entry form and £3 per poem. Poetry manuscripts are not returned nor is any crit offered. Prizes are £60 first and £15 for any other entry published, plus three copies of the issue of *World Wide Writers* in which they appear.

STOP PRESS

Mslexia (March 1999) Quarterly £4.69. Annual subscription £18.75
Editor: Debbie Taylor
PO Box 656, Newcastle upon Tyne NE99 2XD

Because it sounds so interesting and is aimed specifically at writers, a rule-breaking pre-launch mention of a new Arts Council-backed magazine – 'for women who write'. *Mslexia* will be a 50–60 page A4 quarterly magazine with a target initial circulation of about 5,000 copies. It expects to use about 40 short stories per year (up to 3,000 words long), a similar number of poems (max 100 lines) and about 80 articles annually (2,000 words max). Payment rates are £25–50 for fiction, £15–30 for verse and at least £50/1,000 words for articles. *It is, though, only open to women writers.* (Shame.) As well as news items, there are, apparently, to be how-to articles on writing; consumer reports on writing books and courses; interviews with famous writers … and a host of other features. Worth a look.

5

Small Press Magazines

In the past, small press magazines were produced in typescript, duplicated and circulated in penny numbers by dedicated and enthusiastic individuals. Then came personal computers and desk top publishing. As a result, small press magazines have become far better, more professional-looking and easier to read. And ... there are far more of them. Many publish really high quality prose and/or poetry; most are in the market for freelance contributions and some even pay for them. (A handful pay well.) Most small press magazines are still produced by individuals working in their spare time.

Publishing one's own magazine is a risky business though; many small magazines have only a short life. Any listing of such magazines is therefore a risky business; some may cease to exist before the list is published. But, in a Handbook of this nature it would increasingly be wrong to ignore the existence of the ever-growing potential market for freelance writers.

For some of these magazines the classification 'small' may be thought derogatory: it is not so meant. The term 'independent' press has been suggested – but that does not then differentiate between these, often one-person, operations and the much bigger, commercial publications produced *independently* of the big publishers. I am therefore retaining the classification 'small'. Its meaning is clear.

So ... herewith an undoubtedly incomplete list of some of the more interesting small press magazines. In order to compile the list, I circulated questionnaires to as many small press magazines as I could find addresses for: not all bothered to reply - they are omitted. And, in order to include as many magazines as possible, the information on each is in an abbreviated, standardised form.

Mostly, the format is self-explanatory, but a few points need clarification:

- Most of the small press magazines have very small circulations: the circulation groups used in Chapter 1 are therefore not applicable. All the small magazines have circulations in a Chapter 1 category (a). For compatibility therefore, I have subdivided category (a) into:

> a1 up to 100 copies per issue
> a2 101 – 400 copies per issue
> a3 401 – 800 copies per issue
> a4 801 – 2,000 copies per issue
> a5 over 2,000 copies per issue

- Magazines were invited to disclose the approximate number of stories, articles and poems they used each year ... and the approximate number of stories, articles and poems they are offered annually. This information - the freelance writer's *odds* - are listed as 'Chances'; thus, 20/200 means that from 200 offered manuscripts, 20 are used - acceptance chances of 1 in 10.
- The abbreviations are obvious: F = short stories (fiction), NF = articles (non-fiction), P = poems.

Almost every editor/publisher stresses the need for potential contributors to study their magazine before submitting material. Far too many would-be contributors submit *inappropriate* material: it's just a waste of time and postage. And, of course, if you want there to be a small press market for your work, the magazines must be kept alive - by subscribers. Buy 'em and read 'em - don't just write. And always - don't forget the ever-essential stamped addressed envelope.

AABYE (formerly *New Hope International*) (1980), Gerald England, 20 Werneth Avenue, Gee Cross, Hyde, Cheshire SK14 5NL
Circ: a3 Freq: 1 or 2 per year
£3.75 (Sub: £10.00 for 3 issues – cheques payable to G. England)
Uses: P only Size: 60 A5 pages
Chances: P 150/7,000
Pay: NIL; 1 free copy.
Advice: send s.a.e. for guidelines. 'A gathering of talented poets from around the globe; new and old together; traditionalists meet the avant-garde; haiku to long poems; translations; a collage of writing that consistently surprises.'

Acumen (1985), Patricia Oxley, 6 The Mount, Higher Furzeham, Brixham, Devon TQ5 8QY Circ: a3 Freq: 3 per year
£3.50 (plus p&p) (Sub: £10.00 pa) Size: 100+ A5 pages
Uses: F, NF, P. Welcomes short stories (500–1,500 words – not too experimental), articles (500–2,500 words about poetry and poetry-related subjects), poems (any length – if too long will use extracts).
Chances: F 2/30, NF 10/30, P 150/25,000.
Pay: NIL (but may negotiate); 1–3 free copies.
Advice: ensure name and address on every sheet. Decisions on poems to be shortlisted, within 6 weeks; decisions on shortlisted poems take longer; batches of one person's (shortlisted and rejected) poems are held pending final decision/return. Do sample the magazine before submitting work.

The Alien Has Landed (1996), Ariel, Waterstone's, 91 Deansgate, Manchester M3 2BW Circ: a5 Freq: 4 per year
Free Size: 40 A5 pages
Uses: F, NF. Fiction is largely SF/Fantasy/Horror book extracts; welcomes

SF/Fantasy/Horror book reviews (200–300 words max) – but send samples of work before getting too involved.
Chances: NF ?/120
Pay: NIL; as many free copies as wished – within reason.
Advice: Samples first. SF/Fantasy/Horror reviews only.

Alien Landings (1997), Ariel, Waterstone's, 91 Deansgate, Manchester M3 2BW   Circ: a3   Freq: 3–4 per year
£2.00 incl. p&p (Sub: £10.00 for 6 issues)   Size: 70 A5 pages
Uses: F only. Welcomes SF/Fantasy/Horror short stories (2,000– 10,000 words) from subscribers.
Chances: F 24/150
Pay: NIL; 6 free copies.
Advice: Reading a recent issue is the best way to know what is wanted. Try to avoid over-common themes, tired motifs and worn-out cliches – come up with something original and enjoyable. Send s.a.e. for fiction guidelines. Although they do not pay for contributions, each issue of the magazine is sent to relevant magazines and publishers – good exposure.

And (1954), Adrian Clarke and Bob Cobbing, 89a Petherton Road, London N5 2QT   Circ: a3   Freq: 2 per year
£4.00 (no subscriptions)   Size: 32 A5 pages
Uses: P only. Nearly all contributions are by invitation. Does not welcome, but occasionally receives contributions.
Chances: NIL
Pay: NIL; 2 free copies.
Advice: 'See the magazine before submitting – but most unsolicited contributions are completely unsuitable. We are very specialised – visual, concrete/sound, performance/linguistically innovative poetries.'

Aquarius (1969), Eddie S. Linden, Flat 4 Room B, 116 Sutherland Avenue, London W9 2QP   Circ: ???   Freq: 1 per year
£5.00 annual (Add postage 80p)   Size: 150 A5 pages
Uses: F, P. Particularly welcomes short stories – any length.
Chances: F 25/5,000
Pay: 'By arrangement', on publication; 2 free copies
Advice: Policy is to accept work only from those who have studied past issue – and whose work fits style and format.

BBR (Back Brain Recluse) (1984), Chris Reed, P O Box 625, Sheffield S1 3GY   Circ: a4 Freq: 1 per year – irregular
£4.00 (Sub: not available)   Size: 100 A5 pages
Uses: F only Welcomes SF stories, any length.
Chances: F 10/300
Pay: £10 per 1,000 words, on publication; 2 free copies.

Advice: familiarity with the magazine is strongly advised. '*BBR* publishes some of the most startling and daring SF currently being written, and has developed a cult following around the world through a policy of emphasising the experimental and uncommercial end of the form.'

NOTE: the editor of *BBR* is also the contact point for the NSFA (New SF Alliance) which offers a unique mail order service for the supply of sample copies of a wide range of small press magazines from a single address/source. The NSFA catalogue is available free – if you send an s.a.e. – from NSFA, c/o Chris Reed, *BBR*, as above.

Black Tears (1993), Adam Bradley, 28 Treaty Street, London N1 0SY
                          Circ: a2   Freq: 4 per year
£1.75 (Sub: £6.75 pa)   Size: 60 A5 pages
Uses: F, NF only. Welcomes fiction (3,000 word max) and articles (ditto).
Chances: F 30/100. NF 5/10
Pay: NIL; 1 free copy.
Advice: read a copy of the magazine before submitting work.

Cambrensis (1987), Arthur Smith, 41 Heol Fach, Cornelly, Bridgend, Mid-Glam CF33 4LN   Circ: a2   Freq: 4 per year
£1.50 (Sub: £6.00 pa)   Size: 72 A4 pages
Uses: F, NF. Welcomes fiction (2,500 words max) and articles (1,000 words max) from writers born or resident in Wales.
Chances: F 40/80. NF ??
Pay: NIL; 3 free copies.
Advice: everything is Welsh-oriented.

Candelabrum Poetry Magazine (1970), Michael L. McCarthy, 9 Milner Road, Wisbech, Cambs PE13 2LR   Circ: a4   Freq: 2 per year
£2.00 (3-year sub: £11.50)   Size: 40 A5 pages
Uses: P only Welcomes poems from 2-line epigrams to max 60-line poems (but will occasionally consider longer ones).
Chances: P 150/2,000
Pay: NIL; 1 free copy.
Advice: *Candelabrum* prefers traditional verse – metrical and rhymed – but good quality free verse also considered. An s.a.e. is essential.

Chapman (1970), Joy Hendry, 4 Broughton Place, Edinburgh EH1 3RX
                          Circ: a5   Freq: 4 per year
£3.50 plus p&p (Sub: £14.00 pa)   Size: 104 A5 pages
Uses: F, NF, P. Welcomes fiction (3,000 words max) and batches of poems (4 to 10 at a time, not single poems) of any length; most articles are commissioned.
Chances: F 25/700, NF 24/50, P 60/800

Pay: varies (around £8/page), on publication; 1 free copy.
Advice: 'The best in Scottish writing.' Guidelines available for s.a.e.; no s.a.e., no response.

Eastern Rainbow (1992), Paul Rance, 17 Farrow Road, Whaplode Drove, Spalding, Lincs PE12 0TS   Circ: a2 Freq: 2 per year
£1.50 (Sub: £6.00 for 4 issues)   Size: 20 A4 pages
Uses: F, NF, P. Welcomes fiction (500 words max), articles (ditto), poems (32 lines max)
Chances: F 5/50, NF 5/20, P 200/1,000
Pay: NIL; no free copies.
Advice: *Eastern Rainbow* focuses on 20th century culture (particularly SF/fantasy/horror) via poetry, prose and art.

First Time (1980), Josephine Austin, 4 Burdett Place, George Street, Hastings, East Sussex TN34 3ED   Circ: a4   Freq: 2 per year
£3.50 incl p&p (Sub: £7.00 pa)   Size: 84 A5 pages
Uses: P only Welcomes up to 6 unpublished poems at a time (each 30 lines max)
Chances: P 400/2,500
Pay: NIL; 1 free copy.
Advice: encourages first time poets. Send covering letter and s.a.e.: no s.a.e., poems not returned. Donations welcomes, 'to help poetry thrive'.

Good Stories (1990), Andrew Jenns, Oakwood Publications, 23 Mill Crescent, Kingsbury, Warwicks B78 2LX   Circ: a5   Freq: 4 per year
£2.50 + 45p p&p (Sub: £10.00 pa)   Size: 60+ A5 pages
Uses: F, NF Welcomes short stories (3,000 words max) and articles (1,000 words max).
Chances: F 65/2,000, NF 10/150
Pay: on publication, F up to £20, NF up to £15 – amount varies with level of sales of each issue and surplus remaining after expenses; no free copies.
Advice: study the magazine before contributing. Avoid 'experimental' writing styles. Aim at family-type readership.

Great Ideas – a portfolio of business ideas and opportunities (1992), John T. Wilson, Tregeraint House, Zennor, St. Ives, Cornwall TR26 3DB
          Circ: a3   Freq: 6 per year
£35.00 p.a. – subscription only   Size: 32 A4 pages
Uses: NF only Welcomes preliminary outlines/queries for articles (articles to be 1,000 word max)
Chances: NF 30/40
Pay: £20 per 1,000 words, on acceptance; 1 free copy.
Advice: looking for practical articles on all aspects of business and money-making.

NOTE: *Great Ideas* is in a different mould to virtually all others in this chapter: it is of specialist interest and is more commercially produced – but it is neither 'literarily' suitable for Chapter 4 nor big enough to include in Chapter 1. It is worth considering if you have a businesslike mind.

Helicon (1995), Shelagh Nugent, Linden Cottage, 45 Burton Road, Little Neston, S. Wirral L64 4AE Circ: a2 Freq: 4 per year
£2.50 (Sub: £9.00 p.a.) Size: 40 A5 pages
Uses: P only. Welcomes all types of poetry (80 lines max)
Chances: P 200/3,000
Pay: £2 per poem on publication; 1 free copy.
Advice: essential to study magazine before submitting. Standard is high.

Iota (1988), David Holliday, 67 Hady Crescent, Chesterfield, Derbys S41 0EB Circ: a3 Freq: 4 per year
£2.00 (Sub: £8.00 p.a.) Size: 48 A5 pages
Uses: P only. Welcomes poems, any style, any subject (80 lines max – exceeded exceptionally)
Chances: P 260/6,000
Pay: NIL; 2 free copies.
Advice: the shorter the poem, the easier it is to get it in. No party line (except editorial prejudice, which the editor tries to discount), so poets can ride their own hobby-horses.

Linkway (1995), Fay C. Davies, The Shieling, The Links, Pembrey, Dyfed SA16 0HU Circ: a2 Freq: 4 per year
£3.00 + 50p p&p (Sub: £13.50 in UK, cheques payable to F. C. Davies)
Size: 52 A5 pages
Uses: F, NF, P Welcomes short stories (1,000 words max), articles (1,000 words max), poems (40 lines max)
Chances: F 50/75, NF 60/75, P 150/250
Pay: NIL, but prize – which can include free copy (or copies) – for best item in each category.
Advice: stories and articles – any subject; poems – any style. Stories and poetry written BY children are also welcomed (state child's age).

Oasis (1969), Ian Robinson, 12 Stevenage Road, London SW6 6ES.
  Circ: a2 Freq: 6 per year
£1.50 (Sub: £5.00 p.a.) Size: 16 A5 pages
Uses: F, NF, P Welcomes fiction (2,000 words max) and poetry (50 lines max) but not articles (all commissioned).
Chances: F 5/100, P 10/800
Pay: NIL; 3+ free copies.
Advice: look at two or three copies of the magazine before submitting.

Outposts (1944), R. John, Hippotamus Press, 22 Whitewell Road, Frome, Somerset BA11 4EL   Circ: a4   Freq: 4 per year
£4.50 (Sub: £14.00 p.a.)   Size: 70 A5 pages
Uses: NF, P Welcomes poems, of any length, but not articles, which are usually commissioned.
Chances: P 200/50,000
Pay: usually £8 per poem, on publication; 1 free copy.
Advice: read the magazine before submitting. Policy: to publish the best new poetry, by the well established and the *yet to be recognised.*

Peace & Freedom (1985), Paul Rance, 17 Farrow Road, Whaplode Drove, Spalding, Lincs PE12 0TS   Circ: a3   Freq: 2 per year
£1.50 (Sub: £6.00 for 4 issues)   Size: 20 A4 pages
Uses: F, NF, P Welcomes fiction (500 words max), articles (500 words max) and poetry (32 lines max)
Chances: F 5/100, NF 5/50, P 250/1,000
Pay: NIL; no free copy.
Advice: *Peace & Freedom* focuses on environmental and humanitarian issues via poetry, prose and art.

Peninsular (1996), Shelagh Nugent, Linden Cottage, 45 Burton Road, Little Neston, S. Wirral L64 4AE   Circ: a2   Freq: 4 per year
£3.00 (Sub: £10.50 p.a.)   Size: 48 A5 pages
Uses: F, NF Welcomes fiction (3,000 words max) and articles (2,000 words max)
Chances: F 40/2,000, NF 10,1,000
Pay: £5 per 1,000 words on publication; 1 free copy.
Advice: grammar and style must be immaculate. Study the magazine first.

Poetic Hours (1993), Nick Clark, 8 Dale Road, Carlton, Notts NG4 1GT
                                        Circ: a2   Freq: 2 per year
£3.00 (Sub: £5.00 p.a.)   Size: 36 A4 pages
Uses: P only Welcomes poems (40 lines max)
Chances: ???
Pay: NIL; no free copy.
Advice: looking for new poets prepared to write for free – all magazine profits go to Third World charities.

QWF (Quality Women's Fiction) (1994), Jo Good, 71 Buckhill Crescent, Hillmorton, Rugby, Warwicks. CV21 4HE
                                        Circ: a4   Freq: 6 per year
£3.75 (Sub: £20.00 p.a.)   Size: 90 A5 pages
Uses: F only Welcomes short stories (1,000–4,000 words)
Chances: F 80/1,000
Pay: £10 per story, on publication; 1 free copy.
Advice: study at least one issue of *QWF* before submitting work.

Reach (1996), Shelagh Nugent, Linden Cottage, 45 Burton Road, Little Neston, S. Wirral L64 4AE Circ: a2 Freq: 6 per year
£2.00 (Back issues, £1.50) (Sub: £12.00) Size: 40 A5 pages
Uses: P only Welcomes poems (80 lines max)
Chances: P 250/3,000
Pay: credit vouchers, on publication; 1 free copy.

Rustic Rub (1994), Jay Woodman, 14 Hillfield, Selby, N. Yorks YO8 0ND
  Circ: a2 Freq: 2 per year
£4.00 (Sub: £7.50 p.a.) Size: 90 A5 pages
Uses: P only Welcomes poems of any length
Chances: P 200/2,000
Pay: NIL; 1 free copy.
Advice: Jay Woodman's name must be in first line of address on envelope to ensure delivery. Read the magazine before submitting.

Staple (1983), Donald Measham and Bob Windsor (joint editors), Tor Cottage, 81 Cavendish Road, Matlock, Derbys. DE4 3HD
  Circ: a3 Freq: 4 per year
£3.50 (Sub: £12.00 p.a.) Size: 96 A5 pages
Uses: F, P Welcomes fiction (350-7,500 words) and poems (120 lines max – but 'flexible')
Chances: F 30/2,000, P 200/8,000
Pay: £10 per story, £5 per poem, on publication; 1 free copy (but more in lieu of payment if preferred.
Advice: *Staple* never publishes on reputation alone, nor fails to do so for lack of one. Seldom or never holds work over – always need submissions. 'If work is not sent back rapidly, it means we like it, but decision to publish or not maybe protracted. Best times to submit work: Nov/Dec; Feb/March; June/July. Send for back issues (2 for £3) before submitting. *Staple* never knowingly reprints work already published anywhere in the world.'

Tabla (1991), Stephen James, 13a Shirlock Road, London NW3 2HR
  Circ: a3 Freq: 1 per year
£5.00 annual Size: 80 A5 pages
Uses: P only Welcomes poems (any length) in first instance via annual competition (see below) – thereafter, some by invitation.
Chances: P 40/1,000
Pay: NIL – other than competition prizes (see below); 1 free copy.
Advice: send s.a.e. for competition details and essential entry form. Prizes for 1998 competition (published in *Tabla 1999*) were: First £200, and three runners-up, £100 each. First four and other selected competition entrants are published in *Tabla*. Current issue of *Tabla* entitles purchaser to submit five poems for flat fee of £4; other comp entries, £2.50 each. Note: *Tabla* is now formally *The Tabla Book of New Verse*.

The Third Half (1987), Kevin Troop, 16 Fane Close, Stamford, Lincs
PE9 1HG   Circ: a2   Freq: 1 or 2 per year
£5.50 (No subs)   Size: 100 A5 pages
Uses: F, P Welcomes short stories (2,000–3,000 words) and poems (40 lines max).
Chances: F 20/100, P 200/500
Pay: NIL; 1 free copy.
Advice: Please be patient ... and creative.

Weyfarers (1972) Martin Jones, Jefferey Wheatley, Stella Stocker (rotating editors), 1 Mountside, Guildford, Surrey GU2 5JD
                                           Circ: a2   Freq: 3 per year
£2.00 (Sub: £5.00 p.a.)   Size: 36 A5 pages
Uses: P only Welcomes poems (50 lines max)
Chances: P 90/1,000
Pay: NIL; 1 free copy.
Advice: the purpose of the 'rotating' editors is to ensure a variety of styles. *Weyfarers* publishes all styles of poetry but the editors are particularly sympathetic to unusual poems, possibly with contemporary reference.

Writers' Express (1996), Shelagh Nugent, Linden Cottage, 45 Burton Road, Little Neston, South Wirral L6 4 4AE
                                           Circ: a2   Freq: 6 per year
£2.50 (Back issues, £2.00) (Sub: £15.00)   Size: 44 A5 pages
Uses: F, NF Welcomes short stories (1,000–3,000 words) and articles (500–2,000 words)
Chances: F 60/2,000, NF 30/1,000
Pay: credit vouchers, on publication; 1 free copy.
Advice: –

Writers' Guide (1991), G. Carroll, 11 Shirley Street, Hove, East Sussex BN3 3WJ
Publication suspended (Editor deceased).

Zene (1994), Andy Cox, TTA Press, 5 Martin's Lane, Witcham, Ely, Cambs. CB6 2LB   Circ: a5   Freq: 4 per year
£8.00 p.a. (on subscription only – cheques payable to TTA Press)
                                                            Size: 36 A5 pages
Uses: NF only Welcomes articles (500-2,000 words)
Chances: 'good'
Pay: negotiable (minimal), on publication; 1 free copy.
Advice: *Zene* is THE guide (the only up-to-date guide) to the independent and small press scene worldwide – for readers, writers, artists, editors and publishers – providing news and articles, plus contributors' guidelines. Before submitting articles, study the magazine.

NOTE: A subscription to *Zene* would also be a good way of keeping this chapter of the Handbook up-to-date.

Changes to this chapter in this edition

Inevitably, as predicted in the introduction to this chapter, some of the smaller magazines listed in the previous edition of the Handbook have enjoyed a relatively short life – and fallen by the wayside. And I have added a few new-to-me magazines – and wish them a long and happy life. I have also taken the opportunity of the new edition to change the layout of the magazine entries – hopefully to make the details easier to assimilate.

Magazines no longer listed:

Apostrophe
Areopagus
Escape
Metropolitan
Substance
Sunk Island Review
Tees Valley Writer
Threads
Violent Species

and:

The Third Alternative – which has been moved to Chapter 1.

New small press magazines in this edition are:

The Alien Has Landed
Alien Landings
Reach
Writers' Express

New Hope International has been re-christened, and is now *AABYE*.

6

Magazines Excluded – and the Reasons

Many famous magazines are missing from the market-study reports earlier in this *Handbook*. This is because, for a variety of reasons, I do not consider them to be particularly attractive markets for most 'ordinary' – i.e., often spare-time – freelance writers to tackle. This is, of course, a purely personal, subjective judgement. There will inevitably be freelances who are just 'right' for these excluded magazines. Good luck to them. Some missing magazines warrant an explanation though:

Celebrity magazines

A magazine concept imported from Spain, the first of the big, glossy celebrity picture-magazines was *Hello!* – and then came *OK!*. Heavily illustrated, largely in colour, and beautifully produced, the magazines are dominated – to the exclusion of almost anything else – by 'star' features. Interesting to read perhaps, but offering virtually no opportunities for the ordinary freelance writer.

Colour Supplements

The Sunday and weekend newspaper magazine supplements undoubtedly purchase articles from freelance writers – but almost always as a result of editorial commissions. Most of the supplements have a group of freelance writers on whom the editors know they can rely, and with whom they work.

It might be worth contacting an editor if you have a good – and relevant – idea; new writers do break into these markets. But don't waste everyone's time with suggestions that are not relevant to the market. The moral, as always, is to study the market carefully before attempting it. If you can break in though, the payment rates are excellent (but not quite so high as they once were: the recession hit the supplements too).

Watch out particularly for competitions in the supplements. From time to time some of them run competitions: in travel writing, essay writing, 'mini-sagas' (a complete tale told in 50 words), humorous writing, and even short stories. And, of course, photographic competitions too. Prizes are usually large.

Publications with localised circulations

Always excellent markets – albeit often relatively low-paying – every free-lance writer should know well his/her own local county magazine (and newspaper too, perhaps). And if, exceptionally, you have an ideal subject for a local magazine in a remote part of Britain, you can always find the name and address of the nearest county magazine from other, more general, writers' reference books.

Similarly, no freelance writer can conceivably fail to be aware of the local free magazines and newspapers: the 'freebies'. These come through the letter-boxes in a seemingly never-ending stream. Some are reasonable markets for 'ordinary' freelance writers. Be wary, though: not all local 'freebies' pay for contributions. Get that sorted out before you start: if they don't pay, you don't write.

Be aware too, of the *specialist* 'freebies' that circulate nationally. Most of these pay, and usually well. You merely have to find the one relevant to your interests ... and apply your expertise.

Men's general interest magazines

It was long believed that while women happily buy general-interest women's magazines, men would not. Men – the belief was – would only buy magazines about their sports and hobbies (and the occasional 'top shelf' magazine, see below) but not general-interest magazines. It now seems that this belief was ill-founded: a number of general-interest maga-zines for men have been successfully launched. All are relatively up-market, all pay well ... and all are difficult markets to break into. You're up against really tough competition, some of the best in the business. But they're all worth a detailed look if you think you can identify with their requirements.

Arena Monthly. Editor: Eskow Eshun   T: 0171 836 7270
Wagadon Ltd, 3rd Floor, Block A, Exmouth House, Pine Street,
London EC1R 0JL

Esquire Monthly. Editor: Peter Howarth   T: 0171 439 5000
National Magazine Company Ltd, 72 Broadwick Street,
London W1V 2BP

FHM Monthly. Editor: Mike Soutar   T: 0171 436 1515
EMAP Metro, Mappin House, 4 Winsley Street,
London W1N 7AR

GQ Monthly. Editor: Angus MacKinnon   T: 0171 499 9080
Condé Nast Publications Ltd, Vogue House, Hanover Square,
London W1R 0AD

Men's – and women's – 'top shelf' magazines
Mayfair, Men Only, For Women, etc.

The pornographic 'girlie' magazines for men that offer explicit, supposedly erotic pictures and unbelievable tales of sexual exploits are usually – and rightly – still sold from the top shelf in the newsagents' shops. In recent years they have been joined by somewhat similar (but rather less explicitly illustrated) erotic magazines for women. (The introduction of women's erotic magazines mirrors the book world's launching of various erotic fiction lists for women – e.g., Virgin's immensely successful *Black Lace* imprint.)

If you are willing to consider contributing to such magazines, *and will do your own market study*, you will discover that – at least in some of the man's magazines, I can't speak for the women's magazines – as well as the erotica, there are often 'straight' well-illustrated features. The pay is quite good for such articles – well in excess of £100 per thousand words – but the standards too are high, and the work is often commissioned.

There is also a market – in both men's and women's magazines – for what can best be called 'porno confessions' – highly explicit, first-person, stories of extreme sexual exploits. I cannot believe that these are other than fiction – for which, explicitly, there is also a good market. But you must do your own market – and other – research for these magazines. Have fun.

National Daily Newspapers

Although many of the provincial newspapers are quite good markets for freelance feature contributions, the London dailies are, on the whole, not. The 'quality' papers – *Guardian, Financial Times, Independent, Telegraph* and *Times* – occasionally buy articles from 'ordinary' freelances, but the tabloids seldom do. Some of the tabloids though, welcome suggestions and ideas for their staff writers to investigate and write up – and will pay quite well for the idea. This is worth bearing in mind should you have an appropriate idea – a persecuted group of farming nuns or homeless animals or ...

Specialist magazines for the ordinary reader

New Scientist is a very prestigious news magazine – but only for those with a strong scientific or technological bent. As far as possible, it presents 'heavy' scientific information in a form understandable to ordinary people. If – and only if – you have specialist knowledge, and can present it in a relatively simple way, it is a good, well-paying, market. Otherwise forget it.

New Statesman is a left-of-centre weekly which undoubtedly takes articles from freelance writers. Most of its writers though are 'names' or have very specialised knowledge (particularly of social matters).

Private Eye is not really a market for the 'ordinary' freelance writer; it has a style all of its own. It is, though, a good market for all sorts of cuttings or anecdotes sent in by readers: hilarious (but true) news items, misprints, pomposities, over-the-top feminism, boobs perpetrated by radio or TV announcers ... anything like that will find a ready market in the *Eye*. And the pay is quite good. They also use the occasional humorous photograph.

The Spectator is literary, right of centre, all rather intellectual, and largely 'names' only. There are, though, regular, somewhat esoteric, competitions.

Women's glossy magazines:

Company, Cosmopolitan, Elle and *Marie Claire* are not realistic markets for the 'ordinary' freelance writer. They all commission their features from teams of 'known' regulars. Wait for them to contact you – and don't hold your breath. If you have a really good idea, and have successfully worked in this specialist field already, you could try a query letter.

Trade, Special-interest and Hobby Magazines

There are many excellent markets for unsolicited freelance work among the trade/profession, special-interest and hobby magazines. Most of these magazines take a lot of freelance material and often pay high rates. But, generally speaking, you need to be a dentist, an antique collector or a keen fisherman to write for the relevant, carefully-targeted, special-interest magazine. If you are closely linked or involved with a particular trade or profession, specialism or hobby, you will know the relevant magazines (including the freebies) and their requirements – and should already be writing for them (as I wrote in, for example, *Writers' Monthly*). If you are not in the swim, it matters not that you don't know of them.

7

Submissions to Editors – The Basic Principles

There are always new writers starting up, needing to know how to submit their work to editors. Virtually every editor feels the need to remind writers that their work should be 'properly presented' – which suggests that it is not merely beginners who need this advice.

The presentation of your work – how it looks when it lands on the editor's desk – is of considerable importance; it separates the 'professionals' from the 'amateurs'; it is, in effect, the 'shop window' for your wares. Scruffy-looking work creates a bad first impression.

There are certain basic principles about the presentation of work, and also generally about approaching editors:

- All work must be typed, on white A4 paper, (297mm x 210mm) of about 80 gsm weight (not too thick, not too thin). If using continuous sheets of computer paper, remember to separate out the pages before submitting them. (Make sure they're all right-way-up too – and remove the hole-punched edges.)

- It doesn't matter whether your work is typed in *pica* (10 characters per inch) or *elite* (12 per inch) typeface. Any 'ordinary' typeface will do. But don't use 'fancy' typefaces, such as imitation joined-up writing or large and small capitals.

  Most WP (word processor) programs and printers permit you to print your material in 'book-like' type-faces. (This is not necessary, so don't worry if you can't.) Restrict your choice of fonts to something fairly conventional, keep to a similar size to typescript; my personal preference – for all purposes, manuscripts, letters, the lot – is an 11-point *sans-serif* typeface, 'Univers', and maintain the usual double-spacing, wide margins, etc. Most magazine editors do not want ready-to-print ('camera ready copy' = 'CRC') submissions.

  (Never let your ultra-sophisticated WP program persuade or encourage you to incorporate – as some can - diagrams or charts *within the typescript* of an article. If you must include computer-prepared diagrams as part of your submission – and they are not always of adequate quality – provide them as separate sheets, just as if they were photographs, with captions, etc. See below.)

- Don't economise on typewriter or WP printer ribbons: change them frequently so that your work is always easy to read. (You can always, if you must, reuse 'tired' ribbons for personal correspondence or first drafts.) DO NOT submit 'dotty' manuscripts – i.e., 'draft' quality output from a dot-matrix WP printer. Other than conventional typescript, submit only 'letter quality' (LQ) or 'near letter quality' (NLQ) print-out – or use a laser or inkjet printer (either of which are now only a little more expensive – to buy, if not to run – than a dot-matrix printer).

- Set the margins on the typewriter (or WP) to leave 45–50mm (about two inches) on the left and at least 25mm (one inch) on the right.

  These wide margins are to provide room for the editor to make corrections and give instructions to the printers. (If using a WP, many editors prefer the typescript NOT to be 'right-justified' – i.e., they like the right margin left uneven, as with a typewriter. This preference is because the process of right-justifying inserts extra gaps between words which may confuse the printer.)

- Starting a short story or article, scroll the paper (or WP cursor) down about one-third of the page and type the title, in capitals, centrally on the line. Scroll down a further three or four single-spaced lines and type your own name or pen-name in lower case type, again – centred. Do not underline either title or byline. (Underlining means 'print in italics'.)

- Beneath the title and byline, scroll down three or four more single-spaced lines, to about the centre of the page and begin the story or article. Don't indent the first paragraph but DO indent all subsequent paragraphs; maintain a common indent – usually of five spaces. (If writing an article, and providing sub-headings, don't indent the paragraph immediately beneath a sub-heading either.)

- Type the story or article *double-spaced*, that is, with a one-line space between lines of type. Do NOT leave an extra double-spaced line between paragraphs – as is customary in 'office' typing. (If providing sub-headings though, leave a blank, double-spaced, line above and below the sub-head; and it helps if you identify the sub-headings as such by a soft pencil annotation in the left margin.)

- Stop typing at least 25mm (one inch) – preferably more – from the foot of the page. Try to avoid carrying over a 'widow' – half a line at the end of a paragraph – onto the next page. (Carry over one-and-a-half lines rather than the half-line 'widow'.)

- At the top right corner of the second and all subsequent pages, provide a 'strap' (a manuscript and page identification): something like 'Title/Wells/2'. WP users should simply set up a 'header'. The 'Title' on the identification should not be the full title but merely one or two key words from it. Leave one double-spaced line between the 'strap' or header and the first line of the text proper.

- When you get to the end of your story or article, type a short, roughly central, row of dots followed by the word 'END'. Then scroll down to the bottom of the sheet and in the left corner, type your (real) name and address, single spaced. (If using a pen-name, it is wise to indicate this by giving the name and address as 'Bill Bloggs, writing as Belinda Smith.') With a WP it may be more convenient to provide this in a single line, across the page. It matters not, as long as it's there.

- A cover page is a good idea for all articles and short stories. It should repeat the title in the centre of the page, with the *required* name centred below it. Underneath the title and byline scroll down a few more lines and record the word count. I record the number of pages too, saying, 'Approximately 000 words on 0 sheets of typescript.' The word count should usually be to the nearest hundred words – never a precise figure. If an illustrated article, I add, 'accompanied by 00 photographs, by the author, and a caption sheet' (see below). Your name and address (as above if a pen-name) should be typed at the bottom left corner of the cover page.

For stories, type 'FBSR [or 'First British Serial Rights'] offered' in top or bottom right corner. This identification of rights offered is seldom appropriate for articles: it will be assumed – and there are few markets for Second Rights of articles. (See below, for more on Rights.) Articles for the American market however, should always specify the rights offered. They often want First WORLD Rights.

- If you are submitting an illustrated article, you need to supply captions for the pictures. I usually provide these on a separate caption sheet which I append to the manuscript. Some editors and some writer-photographers favour the captions attached to the back of the photographs. It's your decision – or editorial preference.

    If you provide a separate caption sheet, ensure that each picture has an identification letter or number on the back to relate to the captions. Put a name sticker on the back of all illustrations too.

- I believe in sending a brief covering letter with every manuscript. (Many freelance writers do not.) The letter need only say, effectively, 'Here is an article/story about ... If you like it, please pay me at your usual rates; if you don't, please return it.' Letters look businesslike and if you have particular qualifications for writing a feature, are the place to tell the editor so, briefly

- If the manuscript (story or article) is less than about 1,500 words in length and unillustrated, I fold it twice to fit into a DL-size (9 x 4½ inch) envelope. If longer, unillustrated, and not too bulky, I fold it in half. If illustrated, clearly the photographs should not be folded and must be protected with a sheet of cardboard. This, or a really bulky manuscript, may mean using a large, A4-size envelope. Always enclose an adequately-stamped self-addressed envelope *of the appropriate size* with every submission or query letter sent to an editor.

- Increasingly, editors are asking for a preliminary query rather than a complete submission of a feature article – even a short, under 1,000-word one. (This requirement is now indicated in the 'box' on each market-report page in Chapter 1.) A query or article-outline needs to show the editor what the resultant feature will be about, its content, how you propose to treat it, and demonstrate that you understand the specific requirements of the magazine.

    A successful article-outline might take the form of a suggested title, the opening paragraph or two (the 'hook') and a list of the points that will be covered. The outline can also detail any special qualifications you may have for writing this particular feature.

    Many editors welcome – some insist on – photocopies of the writer's previously published work of a similar nature (and in a similar magazine) to that now proposed. (This, of course, makes it even more difficult for a beginning writer.)

Until you are known to an editor, you will seldom get a firm commission for a query-based feature article – but an expression of interest and a go-ahead are well on the way to an acceptance. It is important then to *quickly* deliver what you have offered – and make sure it is up to the outline's promise. When submitting, always remind the editor of his/her earlier interest.

Remember to enclose a stamped addressed envelope with every query. Always query longer articles – say 1,500 words-plus – even if editors don't insist on advance queries; it's to *your* advantage.

Queries are seldom appropriate for short stories – except in those few cases where editors say that they don't want unsolicited fiction at all.

- The most basic principle of all: write for a specific market. Don't write your story or article and then look for a suitable magazine to submit it to. The story-line needs of different magazines vary widely; different magazines want different approaches in their features too. The way to ensure that you hit the target is: first, read this *Handbook*; then, having selected a few specific magazines, study them in even greater detail. When you *really* know a magazine it is easier to produce suitable material for it. And – initially at least – concentrate on just a few magazines to 'attack'.

Footnote – on 'Rights'

When you offer a feature article to a British magazine the editor assumes that you are offering the first British publication of the article. (The 'FBSR' just confirms this.) The 'right', the copyright, is in *the way* in which the facts are presented, not the facts themselves. Once an article has been published – in any British publication, whether paid for or not, no matter how limited the circulation – you can never again offer FIRST British rights in that article. You *can* though, write another article on the same subject, using much the same set of facts, put together differently ... and offer FIRST British rights in that new piece. But DON'T offer similar articles simultaneously. There is no market for second rights in articles; there is, for short stories.

The next three pages of the *Handbook* contain three ten-point checklists – one on writing style, and one each for the content of features and of short stories. Work through the relevant lists before despatch: they should help to improve the likelihood of your achieving publication. (The checklists have previously appeared in *Writers' Forum* magazine.)

10-Point Checklist ... on Writing Style

1   Have you read your finished piece – article or short story – through, *aloud*? Reading aloud helps you identify the hard-to-read and/or pompous phrases that, from time to time, we all indulge in. It will also help you identify subject-object-verb inconsistencies.

2   Are all your paragraphs roughly the same length? Make some of them shorter – the occasional single-sentence paragraph often lightens up your writing. Maybe join one or two 'same-subject' paragraphs together too – to achieve an overall variation.

3   How long are your sentences? If too many of your sentences are over about 25 words, then your writing is probably not the desirable 'easy read'. An *average* sentence-length of about 15 words is a good target. But do vary the lengths within that average.

4   Have you used too many 'difficult' words – ones whose meaning you had to check in the dictionary? (If you needed to check the meaning, so will your reader – who won't bother.) Remember: we're in the entertainment business; there's no captive market.

5   Have you used many 'qualifying clauses' – such as added explanation, like this – in your writing? The sentence containing the explanatory clause is often better rewritten. Keep it simple.

6   Have you 'murdered your darlings'? By that, in this instance, I mean those sentences and paragraphs of which you are particularly proud; the phrases you have written so well. Rewrite them – more simply. Don't try to impress the reader with the quality of your writing. Just 'communicate'.

7   Does your writing still 'flow'? Shorter sentences and paragraphs, while easy to read, can lead to a rather 'bitty', jumpy style. Provide linking words and phrases between paragraphs. These links may only need to be an occasional 'and', 'also' or 'furthermore'.

8   Do the first sentences in most paragraphs – particularly in articles – 'signal' the subject of the rest of the paragraph? The rest of each paragraph should expand on that initial thought. (And, of course, each paragraph should deal with just one topic. You can write several paragraphs on one topic; you should never deal with two topics in one paragraph.)

9   Have you qualified the unqualifiable? Too often, one reads phrases such as 'very unique' – which is rather like being 'slightly pregnant'. Avoid this ... like the plague. And watch out for such clichés. If you must use a cliché, invent your own.

10   Have you gone through your near-final draft and *pruned* it? Most drafts can be much improved by a ten per cent cut. The end result is always 'tighter' – and usually more readable.

10-Point Checklist ... Articles

1   You DID write the article with a market in mind, didn't you? Different magazines will have – maybe slight, but significant – different requirements and styles. You must write for a specific market. So there's no question now, about where you're going to submit it to, is there?

2   Knowing the market, is the article the *right length*? It's no good submitting a 1,500-word article to a magazine that never uses anything longer than 800-word single-page articles. No, the editor won't cancel that advertisement to fit your article in.

3   Is the article as a whole an *easy read* – or does the reader have to work at understanding what you're getting at? To ensure an *easy read*, keep your writing style simple and straightforward – short sentences, short paragraphs and no 'hard' words for which a reader might need to consult a dictionary. They won't.

4   Have you a good title for your article? Keep it as punchy as possible; it's the first thing the editor (and hopefully, later, the reader) notices. And does it give some indication of what the article is about? (A punning title may not initially be clear, but it will become clear after the article has been read; this is fine.)

5   Have you a good 'hook' – a good opening paragraph? If you haven't seized the reader's attention in the first four or five lines, you're never going to get it.

6   Does the end of the article round it all off neatly, tying up any loose ends – and perhaps reflecting the 'attention grabber' used in the hook?

7   Does the content of the article conform to a realistic and understandable sequence; do the comments follow logically, one after the other ... or does it jump about like a flea on a mattress? Fleas are irritating.

8   Does the content of the article live up to the promise of the title and, most important, stick to the point? There are few worse faults in an article than starting off on one subject and ending on a totally different one. Stick to one subject; use the other for another article.

9   Have you gone back over your article and polished it – trimming off the waffle and the repetitions, shortening the over-long sentences, clarifying the meanings? Good articles are never just written – they're re-written.

10   By the time he/she reaches the end of your article will the reader feel satisfied ... or merely sigh and say, 'So what?' Your article must entertain or – in an *acceptable* manner, because you can't force anyone to read it – instruct the reader. Would YOU want to read your article if it were by someone else?

10-Point Checklist ... Short Stories

1   Are the characters in your story compatible with the magazine's readership? It's no good offering a teenage magazine a story about granny – even one of today's swinging grannies – or vice versa. Your main characters should be around the same age as the target readership; readers like to be able to *identify* with them.

2   Is your story the right length? More and more magazines are moving towards the short-short story – maximum length of about 1,400 words. (Individual magazines have their own specific length requirements: a hundred words over or under may make all the difference between rejection and acceptance. Check what they want.)

3   How many characters appear in your short story? There is seldom room in a short story for more than a (small) handful of characters. If you need 'a cast of thousands' ... write a novel. And, a sub-question, are your characters *alive* – or made of cardboard?

4   Have you started the story *late enough*? Short stories can often be improved by cutting out the first half dozen paragraphs. Start as near to the end of your story as possible – at, or immediately before the crisis that leads to the essential *change*.

5   Following on: does the main character *change* – develop his/her personality, overcome some diversity, learn something, perhaps, as a result of the action in the story? The change need not be anything world-shattering – but it must be there.

6   Still on the same general point: is there a *conflict*? Conflict between characters, conflict with the elements, conflict with a conscience, conflict with 'the way things are'? The shorter stories may have only a single conflict; longer stories perhaps more than one. But without conflict, there is no story at all. And the conflict must be linked to the change.

7   Have you described your main character sufficiently for the reader to picture – but without a full biography (for which there is insufficient room in a short story)?

8   Have you included some/enough dialogue? A short story which is wholly introspection or description is usually hard to read. Dialogue makes a story come alive; it lightens up the read. (It also makes a story *look* easier to read.)

9   Does your storyline plot spring naturally from the characters – or is it forced, with the characters made to act out their parts like cardboard cut-outs? Plot should come from character.

10 Does your story start with a strong hook – and end with a *satisfying*, believable conclusion? Does the opening paragraph really grab you? And does the last paragraph leave a good taste in the mouth – without going into unnecessary details?

8

Writing Picture-Story Scripts

Picture-story scripts offer an outlet for the fiction writer that is often over-looked. Both D. C. Thomson and Egmont Fleetway publish a number of weekly magazines filled with drawn or photographed picture-stories; and both purchase scripts from freelance writers. Each picture-magazine uses several picture-stories each week, and there are more than just a handful of such publications. In their usual helpful way, D. C. Thomson will provide interested writers with a whole sheaf of advice on their requirements, and how best to meet them. (Write – with a large stamped addressed envelope of course – to Fiction Department [Picture-scripts], D. C. Thomson & Co Ltd, Courier Place, Dundee DD1 9QJ.)

Picture-stories are much like any other form of fiction: they entail the use of the customary story-telling skills, plus a few extra techniques. There is virtually no difference in the writer's approach to drawn or photo-illus-trated picture-stories: generally speaking, stories for younger readers are most often illustrated with drawings and stories for teenagers are photo-illustrated. The writer starting in this field should, of course, study the market before having a go; it may also help to outline some of the more basic 'rules':

- The writer is not required to provide the illustrations (drawn or photo-graphic) for the story and should not attempt to do so. All that is required from the writer is a script. Picture-stories are told in a specific number of pictures, known as 'frames' or 'panels'; for each frame, the writer must provide all the details.
- Like any other work of fiction, the obvious and basic need is a good story. This needs – even more than usual – to have: a gripping opening, to grab the reader's interest; a strong, uncomplicated plot, complete with atmosphere and a small cast of really believable characters; and a good, powerful ending to the tale, tying up all the loose ends.
- For each frame in the story, the writer must provide:
  - a brief description of the scene portrayed, from which the artist/photographer will work (and see below for more on viewpoint);
  - the characters' necessary dialogue and thoughts (a particularly useful technique this) to be displayed in speech or thought 'balloons'; and
  - any necessary caption (see below).
- Speech, thoughts and captions alike should all be kept as brief as possible. There is no scope in a picture-story for a lengthy soliloquy; all speech and thoughts must carry the action forward. Descriptive

material should usually be *shown* in the picture and therefore left unsaid. It is a good idea to aim at a *total* length of speeches, thoughts and captions in any one frame of about 25 words – and preferably less. Basically, the shorter the better.

- The personalities of the characters in the picture-story should be brought out through the dialogue, the thoughts and the action – not by lengthy descriptions. The captions should be restricted to no more than is necessary to perhaps replace a series of static action-less pictures, or simply to establish the time, for instance 'Next morning'. (Picture-scripts for pre-school 'readers' are different: here, the outside-frame captions usually have to tell the whole story, leaving the frame free of all text. See *Twinkle*, page 73.)

- The description of the scene portrayed in each frame should be as brief as possible. It is best to allow the artist/photographer to use his/her own imagination as much as possible in setting the scene. The photographer will fit the story to whatever is suitable and readily available. (You can have whatever you like, if it is to be drawn – but non-essential detail is up to the artist.) The writer need only say, for instance, 'Close-up: Val is slumped on her bed, weeping'. It is seldom necessary to describe the bedroom and its furniture; Val herself will already have been described.

- When thinking about and then describing the pictures to be drawn or photographed, not only must you 'think visual', you must also try to introduce variety. You can vary both the scene and the viewpoint. (To a conventional fiction writer 'viewpoint' means the character through whose eyes and thoughts the story is seen and told; to a picture-story writer the viewpoint is the position from which the picture is viewed – like a camera position.) If your hero is in difficulties – or thinking – the picture must concentrate on him; the viewpoint you choose will not be that of the hero but that of the artist/photographer.

  The viewpoint can also vary by, for instance, zooming in from a wide-screen identification shot to an extreme close-up of an anxious face. When two characters are in conversation, the sequence of frames might alternate from a viewpoint behind one (looking at the face of the other) to the opposite view. You can select a bird's eye view or a worm's eye view; you can watch your characters approach the viewpoint – or watch them walk away.

  At all costs, avoid a series of frames all with a similar view, with just talk and little or no action. Vary the viewpoint.

- Restrict the number of characters and locations used: remember that each person photographed has to be paid for and that each person has to be transported to each fresh location; if drawn, the more characters and locations, the more imagination the artist has to employ – and the more potentially confusing the resultant story. Ensure too, in your script, that the characters are significantly different in appearance and that their names are not confusingly alike.

- Picture-story scripts should be typed on the customary A4 paper, in double-spacing. Allow an extra wide left margin; in that, type the frame number and alongside, provide the description; beneath that,

119

type the speeches and thoughts, using the left margin again to identify the person speaking or thinking; and when necessary, type 'Caption' in the margin and the words alongside. Usually, restrict each page of A4 to just two frames.

- You can ask for more exotic settings for drawn picture-stories than you can for photo-stories. Period costumes, sun-kissed desert-island settings or crowd scenes cost no more, when drawn, than just two teenagers cuddling on a settee.
- Most picture-story scripts are purchased outright. You will almost certainly be required to sell 'All rights' rather than the more usual 'First British Serial Rights'. Once sold, you will receive no further payments, no matter how often the publisher re-uses the story – in other languages, for instance.

For more 'how-to' advice, Dave Taylor (who writes scripts for, among others, D. C. Thomson) has written an excellent book on writing picture-story scripts, *A Guide to Comicscripting* (Robert Hale), 1993. The book is itself in picture-story form throughout.

Another excellent 'how-to' book has recently been re-published. Although *How to Draw and Sell ... Comic Strips* (Titan Books) 1998, is aimed at the artist rather than the writer, the author, Alan McKenzie, is an experienced picture-script writer and editor and the book offers much useful advice for script-writers too. It also has a lot of useful information on picture-script *thinking*.

9

Writing 'Letters to the Editor'

The beginning writer needs to get into print as quickly as possible – if for no other reason, to give his/her *ego* a boost. Writing 'Letters to the Editor' is one good way to achieve this. No, not writing to *The Times* to say that you've seen the first (or the last) cuckoo, nor writing to your local newspaper complaining about the rubbish in the streets. Rather, write to the editors of those magazines that *pay* for letters. If an editor pays for your letter, you will have sold your first piece of writing.

Many experienced freelances continue regularly to write letters to magazines' 'Letters' pages; it becomes a permanent part of their writing 'business'.

The payment for letters is not insignificant: few magazines pay less than £5 for a letter which need only be a hundred words long. That is £50 per thousand words. There is often also the possibility of a much bigger payment or a valuable prize for a 'star' letter. (In any case, one sold letter per week will go a good way towards paying for a holiday.) And you don't even need any equipment to write saleable letters – not even a typewriter.

Ground rules for writing 'paid-for' letters are:

- The letters should be short and to the point. Forty or fifty words may be enough to gain publication; 200 words will often be over-long. Within those length constraints, get to the point quickly and as soon as it's made, sign off. Make sure though, that the point is clear. (It's all good training for other forms of writing.)
- Be provocative, informative, or amusing; preferably all three at the same time. Editors like letters that stir other readers to respond to them, and if you can make an editor chuckle, you're made.
- Be personal, and original. Forget all the usual advice about avoiding the personal pronoun. Use it frequently: 'I think ...', 'I told ...', 'I went ...'. Write about your own experiences; don't offer second-hand ideas (unless writing about what 'my old gran used to tell me ...').
- Be topical. Don't, for instance, write about Christmas in mid-summer. (Allow for editorial lead times though, just as you would for an article: submit date-related letters at least three months early for a monthly magazine and six weeks ahead for a weekly.)
- Target your letters carefully. Although a general-interest magazine might accept and publish an unusual recipe or DIY hint, a specialist magazine may be more likely to take it, possibly for a bigger payment. But sometimes the reverse applies; so think before you despatch.
- Don't send a letter on the same subject to more than one magazine at

a time. Many editors insist that letters be original (of course) and not previously published. (But that doesn't mean you can't, at some later date, write up the same episode/story in a different way: just don't send them out at the same time – a twelve-month gap will seldom hurt a good story.)

- Wait at least three or four months before you assume a letter is not to be used; you can then try it, or a similar letter, on another 'letters' column.

- Don't try to look like a professional writer. That is not at all what the editor wants, in this context. By all means type your letter if you have a typewriter (and if you're going to be a writer, you must have), but don't use a business letter-heading, and certainly don't double-space. (Do though, leave nice wide margins for editorial alterations.) And if you don't type your letter, do write legibly.

- Don't send a stamped self-addressed envelope or return postage (unless you are enclosing a potential 'happy snap'); don't ask for a free copy of the issue in which your letter is used; don't tell the editor how to pay you. Make your letter look as though it comes from an 'ordinary reader'. That is who the editor wants to hear from; not from a 'professional letter writer'.

- Finally – study the market carefully, just as you would for a feature article or short story. Different editors, different magazines, require different types of letter.

Some magazines also welcome other 'fillers' – brief hints, tips, jokes, etc, sometimes on the 'letters' page, sometimes filling an end-of-page gap elsewhere. These too are good, albeit often small, money-spinners. You can, *if you wish* (but it's not essential), be more professional in submitting fillers: double-spaced typing, several at a time, but no more than one item per half-A4 sheet. Don't forget to put your name and address on each sheet, but don't bother with a stamped addressed envelope – you won't get 'em back.

If you use a pen-name for some of your letters, it is possible that you could experience problems in cashing payment-cheques made out in that name. It may help if you can open a separate – savings bank, say – account in the pen-name. A possibly easier solution is to write your letters using the names of mother, aunts, sisters, daughters, etc. – as long as you can get the money out of them.

For much more advice on all aspects of letter- and filler-writing, see Alison Chisholm's *How to Write Five-Minute Features*, another of the Allison & Busby Writers' Guides. It's great: I heartily recommend it.

Paid-for letter and filler opportunities available at the time of writing, in the magazines reviewed in Chapter 1, are tabulated on the next two pages.

THE BEST 'MARKETS' FOR LETTERS, FILLERS, TIPS, ETC.

(Listed in order of total number used annually – irrespective of payment amount or prize value)

Magazine	Freq	Used annually	'Payment' All	Best
Chat	W	3000	£10 (F £10, pix £5)	£100
That's Life!	W	2500	£20(F £15–25, pix £5)	£25
Best	W	1700	£25 (F £15)	£75
Take a Break	W	1500	£20(F £20–30, pix £25–50)	£25
The Weekly News	W	1000	Nil (F £5/£10)	£10
Bella	W	1000	£10 (F £10–50, pix £50)	£25
Woman's Realm	W	800	£5 (Pix £15, £25)	£25
Woman's Weekly	W	700	£10 (F £10, pix £15)	P
TV Quick	W	700	£10 (F £10)	£25
Reader's Digest	M	600	£200 (F £60, £125)	–
Woman	W	600	£5 (plus £5 for pix)	£25
The People's Friend	W	600	P (Pix £5)	P
My Weekly	W	600	£3	P
Yours	M	600	£3	£10+P
Amateur Photographer	W	500	Nil	P
Woman's Own	W	450	£5 (F £10, £15)	£25
Mizz	2W	400	P – Teenagers only	£20
Amateur Gardening	W	400	P	P
Bunty	W	400	Only for schoolgirls	P
New Christian Herald	W	400	Nil (F £5)	–
Best of British	M	300	Nil	P
Nursery World	W	300	P	–
Twinkle	W	300	P – toddlers only	–
Saga	M	300	£10	£50
The Big Issue	W	250	Nil	P
Practical Parenting	M	250	£10 (F and baby-pix P)	Big P
Prima	M	200	£25 (F £25)	£50
Choice	M	120	P	P
Options	M	120	P	P
Family Circle	M	100	P	P
Home & Country	M	100	Nil	P
More!	2W	100	Nil	P=£20
Candis	M	90	Nil	P
Brownie	M	80	Only for Brownies	P
Geographical	M	80	Nil (Qs and As P)	(Q/A P)
Practical Householder	M	80	£10	P
Woman's Journal	M	80	Nil	P
Good Housekeeping	M	70	P	P

THE BEST 'MARKETS' FOR LETTERS, FILLERS, TIPS, ETC.
(continued)

Magazine	Freq	Used annually	Letters, fillers, tips, etc. 'Payment' All	Best
Ideal Home	M	70	P	P
Mother & Baby	M	70	£10 with baby-pic (F P)	P
She	M	70	Nil	P
Woman & Home	M	60	Nil	P
Essentials	M	60	£20	P
19	M	60	P	–
Active Life	M	60	Nil	P
Writers' Monthly	M	60	Nil	P
Writers News	M	60	Nil	P
Cat World	M	40	Nil	P
Writing Magazine	2M	30	Nil	P
Goldlife	2M	25	Nil	£25

Key: P = prize (of greater value for 'bests')
  F = rates paid for fillers – anecdotes, hints and tips, children's
     sayings, newspaper cuttings, etc.

Notes: 1 An extra payment is usually made – and where known, is
     specified – for accompanying photographs (e.g., with tips) or for
     stand-alone 'happy snaps'.
  2 For advice on whether letters are mostly 'back-issue-related' or
     'stand-alone', see individual magazine report pages.
  3 Magazines with Letters pages but offering no payments or prizes
     at all are not listed. (Again, see individual magazine report
     pages.)

10

Getting Together

Writing is a lonely occupation; you alone can commune with that blank sheet of paper, or the empty screen with the cursor blinking urgently at you. For limited periods therefore, most writers can benefit from the company of other writers. Many people, when starting to write, are unaware of the opportunities for getting together with others at a similar stage in their writing development – or with those who've 'been there, learnt that', and progressed. There are many such opportunities. And most writers are happy to pass on the benefits of their experience – to 'put back' some of what they themselves have gained.

Writers can get together at writers' circles (there are such groups of enthusiasts throughout the country), at writers' schools and conferences, and – in spirit – through the pages of the several writing magazines.

Writers' circles

There are hundreds of writers' circles thriving all over the country. It is almost always worth joining one – or at least trying it out. There are several ways of finding your nearest circle: ask at your library, they will probably know of the local club; look in your local newspaper, they often list their activities; or buy a copy of Jill Dick's excellent *Directory of Writers' Circles*, which lists just about every writers' circle in the country.

Published by Laurence Pollinger Ltd, this is compiled and regularly updated by author/journalist Jill Dick. It is available from her at 'Oldacre', Horderns Park Road, Chapel-en-le-Frith, Derbyshire SK12 6SY. The price of the Directory increases inexorably, but a blank cheque marked 'not more than £5' should still cover cost plus postage.

But a warning: a writers' circle is only as useful as the writing ability, experience – and enthusiasm – of its members; beware the mutual admiration of non-achievers more interested in local gossip than the hard work of 'real' writing. If your aim is to achieve publication – and if not, why bother? – ask about the published works of other circle members.

Evening classes

All over Britain, Local Education Authorities or WEA committees organise evening classes in writing. Once again, the best first contact is your local library. The quality and value of the evening classes will also depend on the achievements and/or teaching ability of the tutor; most are dedicated to the task of developing and encouraging new writing talent. (There are some excellent tutors who have achieved little publication themselves – but are expert at bringing out talent in others.) It is worth investigating these opportunities in your area.

But beware courses not aimed at getting work published. Some courses are clearly and specifically intended for literary study; others aim at therapy. (If you want to become a *published* writer, go for a course entitled 'Writing for Pleasure and Profit' or similar, rather than one offering just 'Creative Writing'; the word 'profit' in the title suggests – at least, to me – a more positive attitude.)

The Writers' Summer School – Swanwick

The five-day annual Writers' Summer School, held each August at The Hayes Conference Centre, Swanwick, Derbyshire, is the oldest-established – and by far the best – of the British writers' conferences. The first 'Swanwick', as it is known by all writers, was held in 1949 and it has been held in the same place every year since.

Swanwick offers five full days of concentrated advice on all aspects of writing for publication. Most days there are two formal lectures – one at 9.30 in the morning, the other after dinner. These lectures are by leading figures in the writing and publishing world; the list of past speakers resembles a Who's Who of Writers.

As well as the main talks there is a choice of half-a-dozen or more courses – each of five lectures – running concurrently throughout the week. The subjects vary from year to year but there is always something for everyone: beginners and well-established writers alike, of both fiction and non-fiction. Some courses include 'homework' during the week – but this is never too demanding.

As well as the courses there are dozens of less formal talks and discussion groups filling the days; there is seldom an empty moment, and usually a choice of half-a-dozen such activities at any time. The last (optional) talk/discussion may not finish until nearly 11 pm – and after that there is (even more optional) dancing until 1 am every night except Sunday.

To get to Swanwick, send a business-sized (DL size) stamped self-addressed envelope to The Secretary, Brenda Courtie, at The New Vicarage, Woodford Halse, Daventry, Northants NN11 3RE. Application forms are sent out in late January; in the past, there was great competition for a place at Swanwick and application forms had to be returned immediately. Nowadays, the odd place is usually still available until somewhat nearer the School date.

The cost is increasing each year with inflation. Expect about £195 for the standard, usually single-room accommodation or about £240 for a limited number of more luxurious twin bedded rooms (£300 for single occupancy of a twin-bedded room). The fee covers full board and accommodation from Saturday tea-time to Friday morning, plus all lectures and courses. Initially, you will get an acceptance receipt – or your money back; the programme, etc. arrives in July.

It is always a stimulating week.

The Writers' Holiday – Caerleon

There is another week-long writers' 'get-together': it lacks the long history of Swanwick but is increasingly popular. This is the Writers' Holiday organised at Caerleon by Anne Hobbs in July each year.

A Caerleon Sunday-to-Friday 'holiday' is somewhat more relaxed than a Swanwick 'school' – nevertheless, much valuable tuition is packed in. 'Holiday-makers' can attend their choice of two (usually from eight) five-session morning courses. There are also many workshop sessions, usually in the afternoons. There are 'one-off' afternoon and evening talks; there is a choice of free excursions to local attractions one afternoon and an 'entertainment' on the last evening.

Accommodation at Caerleon is in single student-type bedrooms; every effort is made to separate (noisy) early-risers from (noisy) late-to-bedders - in separate residential blocks. Food is good.

To get on a Caerleon Writers' Holiday, write to D. L. Anne Hobbs, 30 Pant Road, Newport, Gwent NP9 5PR with a stamped addressed envelope for details and a booking form. Reservations are accepted up to a year ahead against a small non-returnable deposit. Total cost about £250 but increasing annually. (You can try phoning Anne Hobbs, on 01633 854976.)

Other writers' conferences

As well as the longer conferences at Swanwick and Caerleon, there are a number of annual weekend and one-day writers' get-togethers around the country. These shorter conferences are popular with writers and places are often at a premium. To be sure of a place, send a stamped addressed envelope for an application form about six months before the conference date; then, when you get the application form, reply swiftly.

The more important weekends for writers are, in date order:

- South Eastern Writers' Conference: a weekend in March/April, in a country hotel at Bulphan, Essex. Main speakers and specialist lectures. Cost: about £130. Contact: Secretary – SEWA, c/o 47 Sunningdale Avenue, Leigh-on-Sea, Essex SS9 1JY.
- Scottish Association of Writers' (members only) Weekend School: each March at Crieff Hydro, Scotland. Main speakers and competitions. Cost: about £10 for the conference and £120 (separately, to the hotel) for the accommodation. Contact: Sheila Livingston, 36 Cloan Crescent, Bishopbriggs, Glasgow G64 2HL
- South and Mid-Wales Association of Writers' Weekend (if held): probably in mid-May, near Cardiff – but possibly only a one-day Saturday event in the autumn. Weekend costs about £90, Autumn 'day' consid-

erably less. (Past weekends and 'days' have always been excellent value.) Contact: Julian Rosser, SAMWAW, c/o IMC Consulting group, Denham House, Lambourn Crescent, Cardiff CF4 5ZW

- Southern Writers' Conference: a mid-June weekend at the attractive Earnley Concourse near Chichester in West Sussex. Excellent food, excellent accommodation (mostly shared), five main speakers and three three-stream talk/discussion group sessions . Cost: about £155. Application forms available in January from: Lucia White, Stable House, Home Farm, Coldharbour Lane, Dorking, Surrey RH4 3JG.
- Winchester (previously Southampton University) Annual Writers' Conference: a late-June weekend (mainly for beginners) in a further education college in Winchester – with student-type accommodation. A dozen or so workshops/courses on Friday evening and Sunday morning; 60 multi-stream talks on Saturday (Mix'n'match from 12 simultaneous one-hour streams, five sessions in the day.) One-to-one advice interviews throughout Saturday. Most people attend Saturday only. Cost: about £40 for the Saturday alone, add another £100 or so for the full-board weekend. Details, programme, etc., by April from: Barbara Large, 'Chinook', Southdown Road, Winchester, Hants SO21 2BY.
- RNAS Writers' Workshop (Scotland): an October weekend, at Scotland's Hotel, Pitlochry – with lots of fresh salmon on the menu. Main speakers and multi-stream workshop seminars. Cost: about £15 for the conference and about £100 for the accommodation (paid separately, to the hotel). Contact: Les Peck, 38 Ashiestiel Court, Cumbernauld, Glasgow G47 4AU.
- Scarborough Writers' Weekend – possibly in abeyance: a weekend in Scarborough. Seven or eight sessions, each offering a choice of two or three talks and discussion groups. Cost: about £85. Contact, with an s.a.e., to check if it's back in business: Scarborough Writers' Weekend Organiser, c/o Audrey Wilson, 7 Osgodby Close, Scarborough, N. Yorks YO11 3JW.

One-day writers' events abound. There are lots of one-day writing courses (I do some myself, regularly) organised by local education authorities, at around £15–20 for tuition only; but perhaps more interesting to the already-practising writer are the 'Days' and seminars organised by various local writing circles. Watch for announcements in the writing magazines for details. Most cost about £30 (including lunch) and are excellent value for money. Particularly good – and regular annual – 'days', are, again in usual date order:

- Southport Writers' Seminar: September/October, in Southport. Contact: Jessie Mayberry, 30 Kingswood Drive, Crosby, Liverpool L23 3DE.
- Writers West Conference: October, in/near Clevedon. Contact: Pamela Sykes, 17 Old Park Road, Clevedon, Avon BS21 7JH.
- West Sussex Writers Club 'Day for Writers': October, on the outskirts

of Worthing. Contact: N Sheeran, 3 Warwick Road, Worthing, West Sussex BN11 3ET.

NOTE: The contact names for each of the conferences, weekends and days can change from year to year. It is therefore helpful to include the title of the event alongside the person's name on the envelope (and maybe mark the envelope 'Please Forward'); where appropriate, this enables retired organizers to forward the correspondence unopened (and without incurring extra postage costs) to their successors. It's in your own best interest.

11

Competitions

No ordinary spare-time writer – particularly of short stories or poetry – can afford to ignore competitions. They are often the only way – apart from self-publication – that even slightly adventurous poets or 'un-romantic' short story writers can get their work noticed. And the rewards from some of the competitions should also not be overlooked.

The prizes may not be in the same league as the Booker or Trask awards but several offer quite significant amounts of money. And any prize – with, perhaps more important, its accompanying publicity – can be invaluable to a short story writer or poet. It could lead to paid publication elsewhere.

The most important advice that can be given to any writer considering entering a short story or poetry competition is ...

READ – AND COMPLY STRICTLY WITH – THE RULES

and, when sending for details, rules, closing date, fees, etc., ALWAYS enclose a stamped addressed envelope.

Short story competitions

The following is a list of some of the well-established and continuing short story competitions. There are many others that are held just once – for a special occasion perhaps. The short story writer must always be on the watch for announcements of competitions in newspapers and magazines. All the writing magazines (see Chapter 1) publish details of *some* competitions – often including the smaller, lesser-known ones and always, of course, their own.

The three market newsletters/magazines – *Foreword Market News for Writers, Freelance Market News* and *Writers' Bulletin* (see Chapter 13, page 135) – are all particularly good sources for details of forthcoming competitions. (*Freelance Market News* also runs its own occasional short story – and poetry – competitions.)

- H. E. Bates Short Story Competition: annually. First prize about £200. Details: Events Team Office, Directorate of Environment Services, Cliftonville House, Bedford Road, Northampton NN4 7NR.
- The Bridport Prize: annually. Closing date June. First prize about £2,500 (other prizes excellent too).

Details: Competition Secretary, Arts Centre, South Street, Bridport, Dorset DT6 3NR.

- The Gooding Award for Short Story Writing: annually. Closing date end-March. First prize about £1,000. English language.
  Details: Competition Secretary, The Gooding Award, 95 Celyn Avenue, Lakeside, Cardiff CF2 6EL.
- Northern Short Story Competition: annually – for residents of northern Britain only. Closing date end-June. Total prizes about £500.
  Details: Rosemary Jones, Short Story Competition, Arc Publications, Nanholme Mill, Shaw Wood Road, Todmorden, Lancs OL14 4GP.
- The Ian St James Awards: annually. Closing date end-April. 'There is no restriction on length of story but remember that these Awards are for short stories.' All Award winners have their stories published in book form and receive £200. Additionally, prizes of £2,000, £1,000 and £500 are awarded. Detailed, individual critiques available for payment over and above entry fee.
  Details: The New Writers Club, PO Box 60, Cranbrook, Kent TN17 2ZR.
- *Stand Magazine* (see also page 95) Short Story Competition: biennial. Closing date June 1999 (next presumably June 2001). Prizes total about £2,500.
  Details: *Stand Magazine*, 179 Wingrove Road, Newcastle-on-Tyne NE4 9DA.
- *World Wide Writers* (details, page 95): ongoing quarterly, prizes £625 to £125, and annual first £3,125 extra.

Many other publications – all of the writing magazines, several of the women's magazines, occasionally some of the newspaper supplements – also run story-writing competitions from time to time. These competitions are announced in the pages of the magazine/paper – details are seldom released in advance. Such women's magazines as *The Lady* (details, first issue in October), *She* (details, March) and *Woman's Own* (details, October/November) have now held several worthwhile annual short story competitions: the announcements are usually made in the magazines at about the dates shown.

Poetry competitions

There are many poetry competitions – and the prizes are often excellent. The following list is inevitably incomplete. As with short story competitions, watch the writing magazines – and the three market newsletters (see page 135) – for details of forthcoming poetry competitions.

- The Bridport Prize: annually. Closing date end-June. First prize about £2,500.
  Details – as for short story competition, above.
- Cardiff International Poetry Competition: annually. Closing date mid-December. First prize about £1,000. English language.
  Details: Poetry Competition, PO Box 438, Cardiff CF1 6YA.
- Petra Kenney Poetry Prize: annually. Closing date December. First

prize about £1,000 plus a crystal vase.

Details: Petra Kenney Poetry Prize, 21 Belle Vue Street, Filey, N. Yorks YO14 9HU.

- Kent & Sussex Poetry Society Open Poetry Competition: annually. Closing date end-January. First prize about £300.

  Details: Organiser, 8 Edward Street, Southborough, Kent TN4 0HP.

- The National Poetry Competition: annually. Closing date end-October. First prize about £5,000.

  Details: Competition Organiser, The Poetry Society, 22 Betterton Street, London WC2H 9BU.

- Arvon Foundation International Poetry Competition: biennial. Closing date end-November 1999 First prize about £5,000, plus £5,000 in other prizes.

  Details: Arvon Foundation Poetry Competition, Kilnhurst, Kilnhurst Road, Todmorden, Lancs OL14 6AX.

- Peterloo Poets Open Poetry Competition: annually. Closing date 1 March. First prize about £4,000.

  Details: Peterloo Poets, 2 Kelly Gardens, Calstock, Cornwall PL18 9SA.

- Rhyme International Annual Poetry Competition: annually. Closing date end-September. Total prizes about £1,000.

  Details: *Orbis* (see also page 95), 27 Valley View, Primrose, Jarrow, Tyne and Wear NE32 5QT.

- *Stand Magazine* (see also page 95) New International Poetry Competition: biennial. Closing date June 2000. Total prizes about £2,500.

  Details – as for short story competition, above.

- Ver Poets Open Competition: annually. Closing date end-April. Total prizes about £1,000.

  Details: Organiser, 61–63 Chiswell Green Lane, St Albans, Herts AL2 3AL.

- *World Wide Writers* (details, page 95): ongoing quarterly competition, prizes £60 to £15.

12

Addresses Useful to the Freelance Writer

Freelance non-fiction writers depend on information (and personal experience) to keep them writing. And, as mentioned in Chapter 10, they can benefit from associating with other writers.

This chapter lists some useful, but less than widely known research sources/addresses for acquiring information.

Remaindered ('bargain') books

Every serious freelance writer of non-fiction builds up a personal reference library. Inevitably, this reference 'library' contains many relevant specialist books. In search of which, don't forget the various shops selling *remaindered* books – 'Bargain Books'. A book of narrow interest may not sell well, and may therefore quickly be remaindered; but these are often the books of most value to the freelance writer who specializes in the particular subject.

There are two major mail-order retail sellers of remaindered books; both will, on request, add your name to their mailing list. I have dealt with both and had excellent service. They are:

Bibliophile Books, 5 Thomas Road, London E14 7BN (For queries or credit card orders, Tel: 0171 515 9222; Fax: 0171 538 4115; or, 24-hour answerphone, 0171 515 9555.)

Bibliophile charge a flat fee of £2.00 per order (any number of books) for postage and packing – but for orders from outside the UK, add £2 each for up to 10 books (subsequent books in same order, post free).

Postscript, 24 Langroyd Road, London SW17 7PL (For queries or credit card orders, Tel: 0181 767 7421 during office hours; outside office hours, answerphone on 0181 682 0280; Fax at any time on 0181 682 0280.)

Postscript charge a flat £2.50 fee per order for postage and packing for any number of books despatched anywhere in UK/Eire; overseas despatch, add £2 per book (no limit).

Press cuttings

The serious non-fiction writer collects other peoples' articles and news cuttings relevant to his or her specialist interests. A browse through one's collection of cuttings can itself often produce the spark of an idea for a fresh general-interest article. And one can never get enough cuttings.

There are press cutting agencies who, for a fee, will provide you with newspaper clippings of all the reviews of your latest book. These agencies are of interest but little use to the magazine writer.

There used to be just one small agency that offered exactly what the freelance magazine writer wants – the short-term loan of a batch of general cuttings on a particular topic. Unfortunately, this agency has ceased operations. I know of no other source for such general information. (If anyone knows of such a service or decides to set one up, please contact me, c/o the publisher, and I'll be delighted to give it a mention in the next edition.)

If however, you need information on events which, or people who, are or have been, in the news there is another excellent, albeit relatively expensive, source. This is the PA News Library. You can visit them and seek out your own news reports or their own research staff will search for you: either way it's not cheap. Check with them first for availability of material and current fees. (In 1998 they were charging £35 per hour, doing it yourself, or £45 per hour if done for you – in both cases plus photocopying charges of 35p per large sheet, and VAT.) They're very approachable and helpful.

The PA News Library (News Librarian: Katrina Shelley), 292 Vauxhall Bridge Road, London SW1V 1AE. Tel: 0171 963 7000 (exchange) or 0171 963 7015 (direct line). Fax: 0171 963 7065.

Associations

Society of Authors. (Join as soon as a publisher accepts your book, but before you sign the contract.) Contact: Membership Secretary, 84 Drayton Gardens, London SW10 9SB.

Society of Civil Service Authors. (Open to past and present members of the Civil Service and some other public bodies and aims to encourage all forms of writing.) Contact: Mrs J. M. Hykin, 4 Top Street, Wing, nr Oakham, Rutland, Leics LE15 8SE. Don't forget the s.a.e.

Society of Women Writers and Journalists. (Founded in 1894, the SWWJ – as it is known to all – holds monthly lunch-time meetings/lectures in London.) Contact: Jean Hawkes, 110 Whitehall Road, Chingford, London E4 6DW (Tel: 0181 529 0886).

13

Updating Market Information

Whilst no other book offers the same depth of detailed information about potential markets for 'ordinary' freelance writers as this *Handbook* does, even this book gradually becomes out-of-date with the passage of time.

The several writing magazines now published in the UK all provide some measure of market information; these magazines all pay for contributions and are therefore listed in Chapter 1. But there are now three other publications which specialise in offering up-to-date information on magazine markets. Because they are not themselves in the market for freelance contributions, they are not listed in Chapter 1. The three market publications are:

Foreword Market News for Writers: £1.75 per month. (Notional price) Available on subscription only, from: Foreword Magazines, Park Terrace Courtyard, Park Terrace East, Horsham, West Sussex RH13 5DJ. (The annual subscription of £36 covers 6 bi-monthly issues of *Foreword* [the magazine – see page 36] and 12 monthly issues of the newsletter-style *Market News*, and other membership services.)

Eight A4 pages briskly listing new magazines and book publishers and their requirements, existing magazines' and publishers' editorial staff and address changes, news of open competitions – plus some gentle editorial advice.

Freelance Market News: £2.64 per issue. (Notional price) Available on subscription only, 11 issues per year (not July) for £29 (or £17 for 6 issues), from: Freelance Market News, Sevendale House, 7 Dale Street, Manchester M1 1JB.

Freelance Market News has been around, in various guises, since 1968: it always used to be THE market newsletter – but now it has competition.

Sixteen A4 pages listing mainly magazine (but some book publishers) markets both in UK and overseas, giving details of their requirements, editorial staff and address changes, also specific details of (paid) letter and other 'filler' opportunities. News of open competitions – and also of their own monthly competition details and results. (They publish their competition winners – short stories, articles, poetry – in the magazine too.) They also frequently include an in-depth study of one magazine's requirements and sometimes a (bought-in and paid for, at 'rate A') article about opportunities in a specific writing market area (e.g., recently, in-flight magazines).

Writers' Bulletin: £2.00 per issue. Available on subscription only – 6 issues per year (published on the first day of February, April, etc.) for £12 – or subscribe for 3 or more at £2 per issue, from Writers' Bulletin, PO Box 96, Altrincham, Cheshire WA14 2LN.

Compiled, edited, produced and published by Chriss McCallum – author of *Writing for Publication* (How To Books) and a one-time publishers' editor – *Writers' Bulletin* boasts that every item in it is verified at source before publication.

Twenty-four A5 pages listing details of new and changing magazines and their editorial staff and requirements, similar details of new (usually small) publishers, similar details of some of the larger small (independent) press magazines, forthcoming courses and writers' conferences, imminent closing dates for open competitions, and relevant (usually 'how-to') book reviews. There is usually an in-depth review of the requirements of one magazine or publisher. Unlike *Freelance Market News*, *Writers' Bulletin* excludes everything other than competition and market information – no outside articles, no own competitions, no judges' commentaries, no winning poems or stories. It's solid, wall-to-wall market information.

Take your choice – all three are good. And, for up-to-date market information about the small press magazines, don't forget *Zene* (see page 106).

14

The Magazine Writer's Bookshelf

It is always difficult to recommend books for others; others' needs and tastes are never the same as one's own. Nevertheless, there are some books associated with or about writing for magazines that are fairly standard in their acceptance; and there are others that I believe are worth looking at. I list below those relevant books which I think are the best (including – of course – some of my own). There are, naturally, others which may suit you better. But at least have a look at these.

Standard reference books

The Concise Oxford Dictionary (OUP). Many find it too academic but it is the one that I find easiest to work with.

The Oxford Writers' Dictionary (OUP). This supersedes the earlier *Oxford Dictionary for Writers and Editors*. It is very useful in sorting out the preferred choice from alternative spellings and when to use capital letters, hyphens, etc. It is also excellent on punctuation and on printing terms.

Roget's Thesaurus (Penguin). Good to refer to, but avoid over-use.

Collins Gem Thesaurus (Collins). Pocket-sized, quicker to use than *Roget's* (but, of course, less comprehensive); particularly useful too for its foreign phrases, and its list of Christian names.

The Penguin Encyclopedia (Penguin). An ideal one-volume 'first source'.

Everyman's Encyclopaedia (J. M. Dent). Marvellous: try second-hand shops.

The Wordsworth Encyclopedia (Wordsworth). Ideal, and the best value of all – five paperback volumes for a tenner.

Ann Hoffmann: *Research for Writers* (A. & C. Black). The 'standard': ideal for authors of biographical and historical books; useful to all non-fiction writers; more than most fiction writers will need.

The Writers' and Artists' Yearbook (A. & C. Black, annually).

The Writer's Handbook (Macmillan/PEN, annually).

These two annual publications cover an immense range of publications and publishers: therefore only limited information about each. One or the other is essential for every freelance writer: but both need to be supplemented by this – more detailed – *Handbook*.

The Freelance Photographer's Market Handbook (BFP Books, annually). An awkwardly arranged yearbook, primarily intended for photographers but with valuable information for writers too. Worth a close look.

Writing for magazines

Donna Baker: *How to Write Stories for Magazines* (Allison & Busby). Helpful, clear, easy to read. Ideal for short story beginners.

Alison Chisholm: *How to Write Five-Minute Features* (Allison & Busby). Detailed advice by an expert money-making letter- and filler-writer.

John Hines: *The Way to Write Magazine Articles* (Elm Tree Books). Practical advice on article-writing: a different approach to mine (see below).

Chriss McCallum: *Writing for Publication* (How To Books). One of the best 'across the board' books for beginning writers; down-to-earth and practical. Best on non-fiction.

Jean Saunders: *Writing Step by Step* (Allison & Busby). Good general advice on all aspects of writing from a prolific and very successful writer of romantic novels and short stories. Best on fiction.

Cathy Smith: *How to Write and Sell Travel Articles* (Allison & Busby). The best specialist book available on this lucrative field.

Dave Taylor: *A Guide to Comicscripting* (Robert Hale). The only book on the market about writing picture-script – and excellent too. It's all in pictures.

Gordon Wells: *The Craft of Writing Articles* (Allison & Busby). A step-by-step beginners guide to writing saleable magazine articles. The best: and now right up to date in its second edition.

Gordon Wells: *Writers' Questions Answered* (Allison & Busby). Just what the title says. Inevitably, I think it's good, but see for yourself.

Gordon Wells: *Writing: The Hobby that pays* (EPB Publishers, S'pore). I think this is THE best general book for beginners. It is based on 40+ years of writing and selling. (Available from me, direct, at 43 Broomfield Road, Henfield, West Sussex BN5 9UD for £8.50 post free.)

Stella Whitelaw: *How to Write Short-short Stories* (Allison & Busby). More and more magazines are asking for one-page stories. These *short-shorts* require a different technique to conventional short stories. Stella tells all.

Sally-Jayne Wright: *How to Write and Sell Interviews* (Allison & Busby). Excellent step-by-step, practical advice on one of the most important techniques for non-fiction research and writing.

Writing style

Graham King: *Good Grammar in One Hour* (Mandarin, with The Sunday Times). With this book you can pick up on all that grammar you should once have learnt at school ... in a flash.

Keith Waterhouse: *Waterhouse on Newspaper Style* (Viking hb, Penguin pb). Probably the best book of all time on good writing style for newspapers – and equally relevant to writing for popular magazines. A good read too. Get it, even if it takes your last penny.

15

Word Processing for Writers

The debate about whether or not a writer needs a word processor is over. If you write letters and fillers only, or no more than one or two articles or short stories per year, you can probably manage with a typewriter. But if you aspire to sell your work steadily – and with the appearance of professionalism – you have to use a word processor.

(A few – in my view, pretentious – writers may still believe that they need to *feel the words flowing through their arm, down onto the page by pen or pencil* but they are a dying breed.)

Already many magazines welcome manuscripts being accompanied by a computer disk, some *require* it; this requirement will inevitably grow.

Some writers have been 'frightened' about the new technology; these fears are increasingly groundless. Computers – which are the essential component of a word processor – have become much easier to use. You no longer need to learn a strange technological language – all you have to do nowadays is point an arrow and click a button.

The equipment

Word processing equipment consists of:

- a computer
- a monitor
- a keyboard and a mouse
- a storage device
- a printer
- a word processor program

All of the above items, apart from the printer, are usually sold as a single package. (And sometimes even a printer is 'thrown in' too.)

The vast majority of personal computers (PCs) are what were once known as IBM-compatible computers – to differentiate them from the computers manufactured (solely) by Apple. Apple's best-known recent model was the Macintosh – the 'Apple-Mac'. Apple-Macs were long popular in the publishing and graphics world, while IBM PCs dominated the business world. Over time though, the IBM-compatible computer has become more and more dominant: there is vastly more software (the programs) available for it. Most writers today use (IBM-compatible) PCs.

It is useful for a writer to understand the constituent parts of a PC.

The computer

A computer handles all instructions and information as a collection of 'on/off' notifications. Think of millions of switches. A computer 'reads' and 'remembers' each item of information in the form of a sequence of eight on/off switch-instructions (digits 0 or 1, in computer language – or *binary code*). Each eight-digit set is called a *byte*.

A computer has a built-in memory – all those switches – which can be 'accessed'; this is known as random access memory or RAM. Computer memories have grown so much that the memory is now measured in millions of bytes – known as *megabytes* or *Mb*. Fairly 'ordinary' computers may now have 64 Mb of RAM. One Mb of RAM is enough to store a complete 100,000-word novel.

The computer's memory though has to hold more than your words; it also has to hold – readily and instantly available – all the instructions that make the computer work. These instructions are known as *programs*. (In the computing world, this is always spelt without the final *me*.) They include the basic operating system of the computer itself together with the program which enables you, the user, to operate the computer (a *graphic user interface* or *GUI* – nowadays, almost universally, Windows™) and, in our case ... the word processor program.

The speed with which the memory can be accessed and 'worked on' is determined by the *processor* 'chip' – the heart of the computer. Nowadays, many computers use the Intel Pentium processor. (There are other, less well-known processors.) The processor speed is measured in MHz (*megahertz*) – the higher the number, the faster the operation. (Currently, 300-plus MHz speed is readily available.) Older computers used the predecessors of the Pentium – in ascending order of speed and power, the '286, '386' and '486'.

On the monitor

Once a computer is switched on, the associated TV-like colour monitor displays the GUI screen – a number of small drawings (*icons*) relating to different uses of the computer. There also appears a small arrowhead.

The movement of the arrowhead is controlled by a *mouse* – a small movable device which rests on a control ball. As the user moves the mouse – by hand, across a mouse-mat – the movement of the control ball moves the arrowhead similarly on screen. When the point of the arrowhead is centred on the icon representing – for example – the required word processor program, a button on the mouse is clicked and the word processor program is brought into operation. Similarly, the word processor program's facilities – opening (i.e., showing on screen) an existing document, moving individual paragraphs around within it, saving the worked-on document, etc. – can all be initiated by using the mouse.

The keyboard

The words in the document are, of course, fed into the computer by typing them on the keyboard. (It may not be long, though, before voice-operated word processing becomes commonplace. Programs for such computer usage are already available.) A computer keyboard is exactly the same as a conventional QWERTY (the first six keys in the top line of letters) typewriter keyboard ... plus a number of additional keys peculiar to the computer operation.

There is a large *Enter* key which activates most instructions to the computer – and indicates the end of a paragraph when writing. (With a word processor, the computer reads in paragraph-length lines, which it then displays according to the margins you set before you start work. You do not have to move on to the next line – the computer does this for you, automatically.)

As you type your words on the keyboard, they appear on the screen before you. A small, flashing, upright line or oblong, called the *cursor* indicates where the next typed character will be placed. The cursor can be moved to anywhere in the existing text, either by use of the mouse, or by using the cursor-positioning keys on the keyboard. It's easy to add in, or amend, or move words or paragraphs wherever needed.

Storage

At the end of a day's work the computer permits you to save – that is, store electronically – what you have written, ready for continuing to work on it the following day, or whenever. Once work has been saved, the computer can safely be switched off in the knowledge that the work can be (almost) instantly reinstated whenever needed.

Nowadays all computers have a built-in, fast-access, non-removable, 'hard disk'. These disks have vast capacities – up to 5 *Gb* (*Giga-bytes* – 1 *Giga-byte* being 1,000 *Megabytes*) being relatively common today. The operating system, the user interface program and specific use programs such as the word processor are all stored permanently on the hard disk and as such are immediately available. All work in progress is saved – at frequent intervals – onto the hard disk.

As well as the built-in hard disk, all computers have another disk drive accommodating removable 'floppy disks' (inside protectively rigid individual cases, but called 'floppies' because, in an earlier existence, they were) each capable of storing 1.4 Mb. The prudent computer-user/writer saves second (i.e., 'back-up') copies of all work onto removable 'floppies'.

Despite the growing demand for submissions on disk, there will always be a demand for 'hard copy' – that is, your words printed out on paper. To achieve that, your computer has to be connected to a printer.

Printers

There have been major improvements in computer printers in recent years. In the past there were daisy-wheel printers. These operated much like old-fashioned typewriters, with individual characters on tiny arms (arranged like daisy-petals around a wheel) that were struck onto a typewriter ribbon and thus onto the paper. Then, within a 'normal person's' price range, came dot-matrix printers; a number of fine pins projected from a matrix block in the shape of the required character and again transferred the image through a printer ribbon onto the paper. 24-pin dot matrix printers gave an end product which looked as good as conventional typescript. (Output from 9-pin printers looked 'dotty' and gave dot-matrix printers a bad name.) And there were laser printers too – with beautiful output but, in those days, costing a fortune.

Then came inkjet printers, which operate by projecting tiny dots of quick-drying ink onto the paper in all necessary character shapes. The quality of these printers quickly improved and the price dropped. At the same time, the cost of laser printers – which operate like photocopiers, heating powdered ink to seal it to the page– also fell considerably.

Nowadays it is possible to buy an excellent quality ink-jet printer for £150 or so and a laser printer for about £250. Most writers will settle for one or the other. The only disadvantage of these excellent printers over the 24-pin dot-matrix printer (also now available for about £150) is the high cost and relatively short life of ink cartridges or drums (for the laser printer) compared with the small cost and long life of ribbons for the dot-matrix printers. You have to balance the high operating cost against the better quality typescript, etc., produced by the inkjet or laser printer compared with the low-cost operation and limited typefaces, etc., of the 24-pin dot matrix printer.

The word processor program

The operation of the equipment – computer, printer, etc. – depends on the word processor program. Nowadays these enable the writer:

● to insert, delete or move words, or blocks of words around within a document (or into or from another document);
● to draft and print out in single-spaced typescript and then, for the final MS, to print out in double-spaced typescript;
● to 'search and replace' – e.g., to change a character's name from John to Bill – with just a few key-strokes;
● to check spelling and grammar throughout a document (and be offered possible corrections – to accept or decline);
● to vary at will, the layout of any part, or all, of a document – margins, indents, type-sizes, line-spacing, etc., at any time;
● to store, and instantly retrieve, as needed, document layouts, letter headings, commonly used phrases, etc.;
● to access readily and speedily a full or selective word count;
● to print individual pages from within a multi-page document.

There is much to be said for using a 'popular' word processor. For many years I used PSION's excellent but little-known program called *Quill*. I have recently changed to Microsoft's *Word 97* – which does everything *Quill* did and more. (It even corrects my typos ... instantly.)

It doesn't take long to learn to use a word processor. I know. Effectively, I've just done it – with my new program. EVERYTHING was different.

Index of Magazines

AABYE, 98
Acclaim, 11
Active Life, 14, 88, 90–3
Acumen, 98
Alien Has Landed, 98
Alien Landings, 99
Amateur Gardening, 15, 88, 90–3, 123
Amateur Photographer, 16, 89, 90–3, 123
Ambit, 94
And, 99
Apostrophe, 106
Aquarius, 99
Arena, 108
Areopagus, 106

BBR (Back Brain Recluse), 99
Bella, 17, 88, 90–3, 123
Best, 18, 88, 90–3, 123
Best of British, 19, 88, 90–3, 123
Big Issue, 11, 20, 88, 90–3, 123
Black Tears, 100
Brownie, 11, 21, 88, 90–3, 123
Bunty, 22, 88, 90–3, 123
Business Opportunity World, 23, 88, 90–3

Cambrensis, 100
Candelabrum Poetry Magazine, 100
Candis, 24, 88, 90, 90–3, 123
Cat World, 25, 88, 90–3, 124
Chapman, 100
Chat, 26, 88, 90–3, 123
Choice, 27, 88, 90–3, 123
Colour supplements, 107
Company, 110
Cosmopolitan, 110
Country, 28, 88, 90–3
Country Life, 29, 89, 90–3
Countryman, 30, 88, 90–3
Country Quest, 31, 88, 90–3
County magazines, 108

Dogs Monthly, 32, 89, 90–3

Eastern Rainbow, 101
Elle, 110
Escape, 106
Esquire, 108
Essentials, 33, 88, 90–3, 124
Evergreen, 70–1, 89, 90–3

Family Circle, 34, 88, 90–3, 123
FHM, 108
Field, 35, 88, 90–3
First Time, 101
For Women, 109
Foreword, 11, 36, 89, 90–3, 130
Freelance Market News, 135
Freelance Writing and Photography, 11
Free publications ('freebies'), 108, 110

Geographical, 37, 88, 90–3, 123
Goldlife, 11, 38, 88, 90–3, 124
Good Housekeeping, 39, 88, 90–3, 123
Good Stories, 101
GQ, 108
Great Ideas, 101

Helicon, 102
Hello!, 107
Heritage, 40, 87, 89, 90–3
Hobby magazines, 110
Home & Country, 41, 88, 90–3, 123
Home Run, 11, 42, 88, 90–3
Homes & Gardens, 43, 88, 90–3

Ideal Home, 44, 89, 90–3, 124
Illustrated London News, 45, 89, 90–3
Interzone, 47, 89, 90–3
Iota, 102

Just Seventeen, 11

Kids Alive!, 11, 47, 87, 88, 90–3

Lady, 48, 87–8, 90–3
Linkway, 102
London Magazine, 94
Looks, 11

M & J, 11
Marie Claire, 110
Market News for Writers, 36, 135
Mayfair, 109
Men Only, 109
Men's general-interest magazines, 108
Metropolitan, 106
Mizz, 49, 88, 90–3, 123
More!, 50, 89, 90–3, 123
Mother & Baby, 51, 89, 90–3, 124
Mslexia, 96
My Weekly, 52, 88, 90–3, 123

New Christian Herald, 53, 88, 90–3, 123
New Hope International, 106
New Scientist, 109
Newspapers, 109
New Statesman, 109
New Woman, 11
New Writer, 11, 54, 89, 90–3
19, 55, 89, 90–3
Nursery World, 56, 88, 90–3, 123

Oasis, 102
OK!, 107
Options, 57, 89, 90–3, 123
Orbis, 95, 132
Outposts, 103

Parentwise, 11
Peace & Freedom, 103
Peninsular, 103
People's Friend, 58, 87, 88, 90–3, 123
Poetic Hours, 103
Practical Family History, 11, 59, 89, 90–3
Practical Householder, 60, 89, 90–3, 123
Practical Parenting, 61, 89, 90–3, 123
Prima, 62, 89, 90–3, 123
Private Eye, 110
Prosper, 23

Quartos, 111
QWF (Quality Women's Fiction), 104

Raconteur, 96
Reach, 101

Reader's Digest, 63, 89, 123
Rustic Rub, 104

Saga Magazine, 64, 88, 90–3, 123
Scots Magazine, 65, 88, 90–3
She, 66, 89, 90–3, 123
Specialist magazines, 109
Spectator, 104
Stand, 95, 131–2
Staple, 104
Substance, 106
Sunk Island Review, 106

Tabla, 104
Take a Break, 67, 88, 90–3, 123
Tees Valley Writer, 106
That's Life!, 68, 88, 90–3, 123
Third Alternative, 11, 69, 89, 90–3
Third Half, 105
This England, 70–1, 89, 90–3
Threads, 106
'Top shelf' magazines – men's and women's, 109
Trade magazines, 110
TV Quick, 72, 89, 90–3, 123
Twinkle, 73, 88, 93

Violent Species, 106

Weekly News, 74, 89, 90–3, 123
Weyfarers, 105
Woman, 75, 88, 90–3, 123
Woman Alive, 76, 88, 90–3
Woman & Home, 77, 88, 90–3, 124
Woman's Journal, 78, 89, 90–3, 123
Woman's Own, 77, 89, 123
Woman's Realm, 80, 89, 90–3, 123
Woman's Weekly, 81, 87, 88, 90–3, 123
Women's 'glossy' magazines, 110
World Wide Writers, 95, 131–2
Writers' Bulletin, 130, 135
Writers' Express, 105
Writers' Forum, 82, 89, 90–3
Writers' Guide, 105
Writers' Monthly, 83, 88, 90–3, 124
Writers News, 84, 89, 90–3, 124
Writing Magazine, 85, 89, 90–3, 124

Yours, 86, 88, 90–3, 123

Zene, 106, 136